BLAC

NOTES

including
- *Life of the Author*
- *General Introduction*
- *List of Characters*
- *Critical Commentaries*
- *Griffin's Philosophy*
- *Review Questions*
- *Selected Bibliography*

by
Margaret Mansfield, Ph.D.
Department of English
Boston State College

INCORPORATED

LINCOLN, NEBRASKA 68501

Editor	Consulting Editor
Gary Carey, M.A.	*James L. Roberts, Ph.D.*
University of Colorado	*Department of English*
	University of Nebraska

ISBN 0-8220-0245-0
© Copyright 1971
by
Cliffs Notes, Inc.
All Rights Reserved
Printed in U.S.A.

2000 Printing

Cliffs Notes, Inc.   Lincoln, Nebraska

CONTENTS

Black Like Me Notes

LIFE OF THE AUTHOR

On first learning the theme of *Black Like Me,* most people find it remarkable that a Southern white would change the color of his skin and become a black man, even for a few weeks. Was he motivated, they wonder, by curiosity—a desire to experience as many sides of life as possible? Was it simply that he was paid very well for his account of his experiences as a black man? Or was this an extraordinary man—one possessing a rare amount of compassion and courage—who sincerely wished to understand and to communicate to other whites the true effects of their racism on the day-to-day life of blacks?

The details of John Howard Griffin's life make it hard to believe that he became a black man simply because of vulgar curiosity or a desire for money. In fact, the story of his life is that of a highly learned man who was able to overcome most of the prejudices ingrained in him by his Texas upbringing, and who became intensely dedicated to the cause of racial justice in a society which despised and threatened him for his efforts.

Griffin was born in Dallas, Texas, on June 16, 1920, and grew up in the Dallas-Fort Worth area. Under the influence of his mother, a concert pianist, he developed an early love of music which was to remain with him all his life. At sixteen, he went to France, where he completed his secondary education in 1938. Since Griffin had decided to become a psychiatrist, he began to study medicine and psychiatry at the Medical School of Tours, spending part of his time as an assistant to the director of an insane asylum in that city. But his involvement with music was too much a part of himself to be ignored, and his experiments with music as therapy for the insane led him to continue his study of musical composition, theory, and history.

During World War II, Griffin worked with the French underground movement, aiding in the escape of German and American refugees; later he joined the United States Army, fighting in the South Pacific and the Far East. The war interrupted his studies in both psychiatry and music, and severe damage to his eyesight as a result of war injuries put an end to his hopes of being a psychiatrist. He did continue his musical studies, however, and these were eventually to make him a recognized authority on certain aspects of music, most notably the Gregorian chant.

In 1947, Griffin, now totally blind, returned to Mansfield, Texas, where he took up cattle ranching while learning Braille and other skills necessary to the sightless. His return emphasized the fact that two major changes in values had taken place during his eleven-year absence. The first was an increasing attraction to Roman Catholicism, largely resulting from the influence of the priests and brothers in the French monastery where Griffin had studied music just before and after he went totally blind. His first novel, *The Devil Rides Outside,* written in 1952, draws upon this experience and centers on a young man's gradual rejection of worldly and sensual pursuits in favor of spiritual commitment. Griffin has acknowledged that writing this novel was a key factor in his own conversion to Catholicism, which occurred the same year.

The second major change involved a total reassessment of Griffin's social values. As a teenager in France, he had rapidly become aware that his schoolmates there did not share his Texas-bred sense of superiority to Negroes or his distaste for associating with black people on an equal basis. Moreover, as he witnessed the growth of Nazi anti-Semitism in pre-World War II Europe, he found inescapable parallels to the attitudes of whites toward blacks in his own country. It became obvious to him that one of America's major problems was racism.

In 1957, Griffin's eyesight suddenly returned, and in the following years he became prominent as a syndicated newspaper columnist. His increasing commitment to change Southern racist attitudes through his journalistic writings culminated in the experiences narrated in *Black Like Me,* first serialized in *Sepia* magazine in 1960.

In the journals he wrote before undertaking this racial transformation and in the early parts of the book itself, Griffin speaks of his conviction that he must follow through with this project, even though he seriously feared reprisals. Unfortunately, when his account was published, his fellow Texans' reactions surpassed even his worst estimates of the malignant hatred festering in Southern white minds. Griffin, his wife, their four children, and Griffin's parents all became targets for threats of death or mutilation. Members of the black community secretly kept watch on the Griffin house to prevent violence. Finally, fearful for his family's safety and intensely saddened by his fellow whites' hatred and bigotry, Griffin moved his household to Mexico, where they remained until political unrest and anti-American sentiment forced them to leave. The Griffin family later returned to Texas and now resides in Fort Worth.

Besides the works already discussed, Griffin has written another novel, *Nuni* (1956); *Land of the High Sky* (1959), a history of western Texas and its Indian culture; a number of short stories; and many articles dealing with such topics as music, racism, primitive cultures, censorship, and religion. He is currently working on several books, including an autobiography to be titled *Scattered Shadows.* Griffin has also gained recognition in the field of photography and has done portraits of many prominent contemporary figures. He has received numerous awards for his various writings, including the Christian Culture Award, a citation from the National Association of Negro Women, and the *Pacem in Terris* Award established by Pope John XXIII.

GENERAL INTRODUCTION

RACISM: DEFINITION AND HISTORY

Fundamental to the understanding of race relations in this country is a comprehension of the term *racism*. Basically, racism is the conviction that another race is innately inferior to one's own or to all other races, and that it is therefore morally right to segregate, to dominate, and even to eliminate that race. Racism takes for granted such generalizations as "All Negroes are lazy." A racist accepts at face value a certain line of reasoning ("Since this man is a 'nigger' he must be lazy") and a certain emotional attitude ("I hate those lazy niggers").

Modern scientific and psychological studies have proven, however, that there is no evidence that the Negro race is biologically, intellectually, or temperamentally inferior to any other race. Yet myths about the Negro's inferiority and his "animalistic" nature are still popularly believed—for example, that the black man's brain is smaller than the white man's, that his sexual organs are larger, that he is lazier, less intelligent, and more inclined to criminal acts. Not only are accusations of this sort untrue, but modern sociologists and anthropologists also question whether there are any objective criteria—apart from superficial or cultural ones—for classifying human beings as belonging to one race rather than another. Certainly there is no historical or scientific basis for a concept of racial "purity" which insists that anyone who is not one hundred percent Caucasian (an unprovable issue in itself) belongs to a totally different race.

Why, then, did such misconceptions develop in the first place? The recent work of historians and sociologists has suggested that the roots of such racist beliefs lie early in the era when the white man in this country was enslaving black people. At first, black slaves were treated quite similarly to white indentured servants,* but as it became economically more profitable to push some slaves into lower and lower conditions and to refuse them the indentured man's privilege of working off his bondage, blacks were singled out for such suppression. A man who wished to enslave others—as opposed to using their services as indentured men—knew that it would be considered

---

*An indentured servant was one who signed a bond or a contract to work as an apprentice or servant. Usually some arrangement was made either to set a specific time limit for this service or to allow the indentured man or woman to use gifts or earnings to "buy off" his indenture after a minimum period of service.

immoral to deprive men just like himself of their fundamental rights. Thus, he sought out people of a culture and appearance different from his own; he believed that he could classify them at least as "inferior" human beings, or even, with a little more rationalization, as "subhuman." This categorization enabled him to justify his enslavement of them: in his mind they were like cattle or horses — inferior creatures created for the use of superior beings like himself.

When slavery was legally abolished, the white former slave-owner either had to accept and acknowledge the idea that he had been wrong in his practices or he had to work even harder than before to convince himself that he had, after all, only been exerting the natural domination of a superior creature over an inferior one. The latter train of thought seems to be the basis for contemporary Southern racism. Of course, the more the freed slaves tried to raise their level of accomplishment — the more they threatened to show themselves as equals of whites in every way — the more the white racist had to prevent such achievements in order to prevent a feeling of guilt. Thus, a vicious circle was created which lasts still today: the more the white man oppressed Negroes, the greater guilt he felt, and, therefore, the more he had to oppress blacks in order to prove to himself that blacks were inferior.

Nor was the Northerner free of such racist views, although his actions and policies were not so extreme. Once the zeal of the antislavery movement had been tempered by the Northern victory in the Civil War and by the granting of citizenship and voting rights to Negroes shortly afterward, the Northerner found it easier simply to sit back and let the South work out its own problems. Without the prodding of the Northern conscience, Southern white racism grew more vindictive than ever in the last three decades of the nineteenth century. The degree of repression and the number of mob actions against Negroes reached a peak in the South around the turn of the century — a period when a hundred or more lynchings a year were common. And from the 1880s on, the South enacted various laws designed to achieve the complete segregation of blacks from whites. As a result of their failure to stop these outrages, and also because of their toleration of increasingly worse conditions in their own ghettos, Northerners began to feel guilty. Thus, they too began to subscribe to some of the Southern theories of black racial inferiority in order to justify their own lack of responsibility.

In the first half of this century, problems persisted in the South and grew more acute in the North. Large numbers of blacks migrated to cities in the North only to find that they had exchanged rural poverty for urban poverty. With virtually no financial resources, the migrant blacks found they could afford to live in only the most dilapidated areas of the cities. Moreover, the Northern whites, while unwilling to approve segregationalist laws, were not receptive to the influx of large numbers of unskilled workers unused to urban living. The new group had a different way of life and, moreover, was an economic threat to the low income whites because they could be exploited by unscrupulous employers who could hire them at lower wages. White workers, generally poorly educated, were quick to adopt many of the racist attitudes of Southerners, espousing the doctrine of the inferiority of the Negro race in order to discourage employers from hiring black workers who, whites insisted, might work for lower wages but were too lazy and stupid to work as well as they. As these white workers improved themselves economically and moved into the suburbs, they took their racist attitudes with them, creating the white belt around the central urban area, a pattern typical of most Northern cities today.

Black Northern ghettos became centers of frustration and despair; first, because of the intolerable living conditions produced by overcrowding, and by the unwillingness of cities to spend money to improve ghetto schools and facilities, to provide adequate public services, and to enforce building codes and health regulations against unprincipled white landlords; and, second, because even a successful black was prevented by white society and by unscrupulous realtors from moving into better neighborhoods.

In the North, then, despite liberals' condemnations of Southern bigotry and proclamations of equal rights for all races, economic patterns were such that a Negro in an urban ghetto was virtually predestined to a life of poverty, disease, and social restriction. Unlike the South, however, the North did tolerate some blacks in professional fields and did allow occasional token integration of a few schools and neighborhoods.

In the North, social restraints involved subtle tactics, but Southerners did not hesitate to indulge in the most flagrant violations of law to repress Negroes. Virtually all blacks were prevented from registering to vote; all were in segregated schools, usually greatly inferior ones specifically designed to keep the educational level of Negroes low; and all were prohibited from using the same public facilities as whites. Furthermore, blacks lived in constant fear of the brutality of public officials and the violence of white mobs.

World War II had two important effects on race relations in the United States. First, many Negroes returned to this country after having found an acceptance abroad which was denied to them in this country. When they returned to America's racist restrictions, these blacks were understandably less willing to tolerate such injustice. This unwillingness led to increasingly organized efforts by blacks to achieve their civil rights; they established CORE (Congress of Racial Equality) in the early 1940s and revitalized such existing organizations as the NAACP (National Association for the Advancement of Colored People) and the National Urban League. The movement continued with the efforts of Martin Luther King, Jr. and others in the Montgomery bus boycotts and later in the 1957 establishment of the SCLC (Southern Christian Leadership Conference). Currently, of course, disillusioned with the ability of such nonviolent organizations to achieve necessary changes, black protest has taken on a more militant aspect in such newer organizations as the Black Panthers; in the reassessment of tactics and goals by such older organizations as SNCC (Student Nonviolent Coordinating Committee) and CORE; and in the formation of various black students' organizations.

The second important effect of the war on race relations was that because of its role in the war, the United States had world attention strongly focused on it. Suddenly Northern liberals began to become conscious of the ugly image which American racism gave this country abroad. These influences combined in the 1950s to produce a reawakening of the Northern liberal conscience which—added to the effects of the Negro civil rights movement—resulted in the passage of certain beneficial legislation and in several crucial Supreme Court decisions. But the outcome of this period of reform was not enough to prevent such later occurrences as the outbreaks in Watts and Jersey City, the discriminatory law enforcement tactics visible in the Jackson State incident, and the considerable white backlash of the present time.

THE SOUTH IN 1959

John Howard Griffin's journey as a Negro through parts of the Deep South took place in late 1959, a time when many whites —in the North, at least—were congratulating themselves on their increasingly liberal attitudes on race and were looking with satisfaction at the record of legislative progress toward full equality for blacks. On paper, a brief survey of civil rights legislation in the 1950s looks quite good: it includes the Supreme Court's 1954 school desegregation order, its 1956 ruling on desegregating buses in Montgomery and other Southern cities, and the establishment in 1957 of the Civil Rights Commission, empowered to investigate charges of discrimination throughout the country. And legally, of course, blacks had had the right of citizenship and the right to vote since the passage of the fourteenth and fifteenth amendments in 1866 and 1870.

But any native Southerner, black or white, knew that there was a vast difference between the actual and the paper status of Negroes in the late 1950s. Most Supreme Court decisions were either ignored or evaded. The 1961 Freedom Rides* to Alabama

*Freedom Rides began as a test of the Interstate Commerce Commission order against segregation in interstate buses and terminals. CORE and also the Nashville Student Movement organized and carried out the rides, during which Negroes occupied seats traditionally denied to them in the front of the bus. The Freedom Riders were several times the victims of white mob violence, and over fifty of the Riders were jailed for their participation in the protests.

and Mississippi, for example, dramatized the persistence of bus segregation in flagrant defiance of the 1956 decision. Blacks were kept out of white schools by any means available, a frequent tactic being the maneuvering of boundaries to keep school districts racially distinct. Constitutional guarantees were also sidestepped, and especially in Alabama and Mississippi, outlandish literacy tests and various forms of intimidation were used to keep blacks from registering to vote.

Griffin's conversations with Southern blacks and his observation of their life from within clearly reveal the ruthless and extra-legal campaign to keep "niggers in their place." He personally experiences the indignities of segregated buses, rest rooms, eating places, and hotels. His job inquiries are fruitless despite his outstanding education; as one plant foreman tells him, "We don't want you people. Don't you understand that?" And he sees evidence everywhere around him of the crippling effects of subhuman living conditions and inferior schools on the spirits of black men.

In the final analysis, however, it is not the specific violations of law, or denials of basic rights which are most appalling to Griffin. Rather, it is the racist's refusal to acknowledge blacks as human beings. It is such a refusal that allows otherwise upstanding citizens (like some of the drivers who pick up the hitchhiking Griffin) to believe that they are doing Negro women a favor by having sexual relations with them, but that it is forbidden for a black man even to look at a white woman. It is such an attitude, too, that allows whites to see blacks as commodities so that any one of "them" is always expendable — especially when a lynching or a beating may "teach them to keep in their places."

Racism, in fact, seems to Griffin so deeply engrained not only in the Southern but also in the Northern white outlook that it permeates the attitudes of even those who think themselves enlightened. In its subtler forms, racism reveals itself in unconscious condescension rather than in overt malice. It is entrenched in the attitude of the educated young man who gives

Griffin a ride in Alabama: despite his supposed admiration of Negroes' "healthier" sexual views, he unwittingly reveals to the journalist that he considers blacks basically animalistic; and he is utterly astonished that his passenger, whom he takes to be black, can speak intelligently. Unconscious racism also shows itself when the Southern white on the bus to Georgia states that he would have prevented a white bully from striking a black man, but involuntarily refers to the black man by the condescending term "boy." Still another variation appears in the behavior of the Ph.D. from New York who patronizingly offers to buy all of an elderly Negro vendor's turkeys. He so resents the old man's refusal to take part in this "charitable" act that he concludes, "There's something 'funny' about all of you."

There is little doubt, then, that in the South of 1959 racist views and policies continued, in effect, to enslave the black man.

GRIFFIN'S PURPOSE

Why did Griffin undertake this project? Why did he feel that it was necessary to disguise himself as a Negro rather than simply listening to what black men themselves had to say about the conditions of their life in the South? The answer lies in the very thickness of the barrier which racism has erected between blacks and whites.

Griffin is, after all, writing to tell whites about what they are doing to blacks. He believes that most whites cannot realize the sheer inhumanity of their attitudes and policies — and that if they were made to realize this, they might change. (Griffin later becomes disillusioned with the idea that such an approach could produce change quickly enough; see the Bradford Daniel interview in the bibliography.) The people Griffin hopes to reach with *Black Like Me* would not believe the testimony of a Negro — after all, American black writers have been depicting the effects of repression on their people since slave days, and most whites have never even bothered to read their works. Moreover, the racism of whites in the South of 1959 was such that if *Black*

Like Me were the work of a real Negro—and if it were widely read—its revelations and accusations would, at best, be ignored or dismissed as exaggerations or lies; at worst, they could provoke some sort of repressive, punitive, or directly violent action toward the author—probably much more vindictive than the threats leveled against Griffin.

Moreover, because of these very hostilities, Griffin as a white reporter would have little hope of gaining true information from the blacks he interviewed. Negroes in the South long ago learned the wisdom of telling the white man only what he wanted to hear—and even the best intentioned Southern whites wanted to hear that blacks were basically happy, that things weren't so bad. For if a decent white was confronted with the truth and accepted it, he would have to make the agonizing choice between the hypocrisy of keeping silent and the dangers to himself and his family of speaking out in a society dominated by racist hatred. So blacks, recognizing the degree to which white men might go to preserve this comfortable ignorance, chose to conceal the facts of their misery rather than risk further repression.

Furthermore, Negroes would be understandably suspicious of the motives of a white reporter asking them such questions as Griffin might ask. It was not uncommon for a sadistic white to gain the confidence of a Negro, lead him into making certain statements about those who were oppressing or threatening him, and then beat him up or take away his job for being "uppity" enough to tell "lies about our upstanding citizens." It is the well-founded fears of tactics like these which make Negroes reluctant to pose for Don Rutledge, the white photographer, in the latter part of the narrative. Obviously Griffin, had he posed as a white reporter, would never have gained a true notion of what life is like for Southern blacks.

For these reasons, then, Griffin undertakes this experiment and writes *Black Like Me,* despite the personal risks. It is a book about black people, written by a white man for a white audience, and should in no sense be classified as "black literature." But it is an important text for whites who wish to begin learning about their own racism, about the repressive practices of the society their race dominates economically and politically, and about the fundamental reasons for black protest. In fact, for a white reader, *Black Like Me* is not a bad preliminary to the study of black literature itself.

LIST OF CHARACTERS

NAMED CHARACTERS

John Howard Griffin

Author and main character, a white Texas novelist, journalist, and rancher who temporarily darkens his skin in order to find out what life is like for a Negro in the South.

George Levitan

Owner of *Sepia*, a popular Negro magazine; he agrees to finance Griffin's project in return for articles for his publication.

Mrs. Adelle Jackson

Editorial director of *Sepia* who warns Griffin of the probable hostility of Southern whites to his project.

Sterling Williams

Elderly black shoeshine "boy" who becomes Griffin's contact for entry into the black community in New Orleans.

Joe

Williams' partner in the shoeshine business.

Reverend A. L. Davis, Mr. Gayle, and J. P. Guillory

Educated and influential members of the New Orleans black community. They meet daily at the Y Coffee Shop to eat and exchange ideas. Griffin's conversations with the men provide him with valuable insights into the problems of Negroes in that city.

Christophe

Handsome, well-educated Negro whom Griffin meets on the bus to Hattiesburg, Mississippi. The frustrations of being black in a racist society have led him to despise his own race and to adopt a life of crime.

Bill Williams

Young black on the bus to Hattiesburg who tells Griffin the details of the Mack Parker lynching and helps him to find a place to stay in the city.

P. D. East

Mississippi newspaper editor and friend with whom Griffin stays in Hattiesburg. East has jeopardized the financial success of his newspaper and suffers social ostracism because of his outspoken campaign for racial justice.

Billie East

P. D.'s wife.

Dean Sam Gandy

Dean of Dillard, a black university in New Orleans, visited by East and Griffin.

T. M. Alexander

Black businessman and leader in Atlanta who represents, to Griffin, the Negro community's successful efforts toward economic, educational, and social advancement.

Don Rutledge

White photographer who accompanies Griffin to Atlanta and New Orleans for a *Sepia* assignment.

UNNAMED CHARACTERS

The dermatologist who gives Griffin skin-darkening treatments

His experiences with blacks in seamy sections of New Orleans have left him with the impression that Negroes have a destructive attitude toward their own race.

The well-educated, young white driver who picks Griffin up in Alabama

He believes that the Negro is a different species than himself, lacking in his own emotional sensitivity and moral principles, but endowed with great sexual powers.

The young white construction worker who gives Griffin a ride into Mobile

The only white Griffin encounters during his hitchhiking who seems totally free of hatred and racial prejudice.

The elderly black preacher who invites the journalist to bunk with him in Mobile

He believes Christian love obligates him to love even those whites who hate and persecute him for being black.

The white Alabama grandfather and civic leader who gives Griffin a ride through the swamp country between Mobile and Montgomery

His racism is so acute that he sees a white man's promiscuity with black women as doing the "niggers" a favor by giving some of their children a little white blood.

The young black sawmill worker who takes Griffin into his two-room shanty in the Alabama swamps

This courageous father of six represents to Griffin black people's struggle for a decent and loving family life in the midst of incredibly oppressive circumstances.

The white Ph.D. from New York whom Griffin meets near Tuskegee Institute in Montgomery

Despite his good intentions, he embarrasses both Griffin and an elderly turkey vendor by his patronizing "white liberalism."

The guestmaster at the Trappist monastery in Georgia

He laments to the journalist the hypocritical religiosity of many racists.

CRITICAL COMMENTARIES

Because *Black Like Me* is not a work of fiction, and because it is presented to us as a chronological journal, the book does not fall into the kind of homogeneous chapter or section divisions that are usually found in novels. Yet John Howard Griffin, a novelist as well as a journalist, does manage to present his story to us in a fairly well defined pattern. His account of his transformation, his experiences in New Orleans, and his bus trip to Mississippi build to a dramatic climax of despair in the desolate hotel room in Hattiesburg. There he finds himself unable to bear any longer his sense of utter loneliness. There is an interlude — in part, a sort of comic relief for his tensions and hopelessness — when Griffin visits his friend P. D. East. After this interlude, Griffin renews his journey, pushing both geographically and psychologically further into the depths of the Deep South — Mississippi and Alabama. A kind of turning point, the beginning of a glimmer of light, is provided by the optimistic atmosphere in

Montgomery as a result of the efforts of Martin Luther King, Jr. and his followers. From this point on, the narrative begins to be more fragmented as Griffin switches back and forth between his black and white identities. Finally, we are given a kind of epilogue as the author tells us of the hostile reactions of his neighbors and fellow townsmen in Texas and of his decision to move his family to Mexico.

PART I: PRELIMINARIES (MANSFIELD, TEXAS, AND NEW ORLEANS; OCTOBER 28-NOVEMBER 6)

What would it be like to be a Negro in the Deep South? It is this question which begins Griffin's narrative and which is meant to sum up his motivation for his extraordinary project. For several years Griffin's journalistic efforts had been directed at the so-called race problem, and when his narrative begins he is engaged in a scientific research study of the condition of Negroes in the South, to be backed up by statistics which supposedly could provide an objective measure of the suffering of a whole race. In the first journal entry, we learn that the author has just finished reading a report documenting the rise of the suicide tendency among Southern Negroes — that is, an increase not in the number of people who have taken and are taking their own lives, but in the number who do not care whether they live or die. It is at this point that Griffin recognizes that, for the reasons already discussed, a white man can never really know the truth about Negro life, nor can he feel personally these black men's hopeless denials of the value of living. For there are too many lies; there is too much hostility and suspicion. Griffin comes to the only possible conclusion: if he wants to learn what Negro life is really like, he must become a black man.

In Fort Worth, when Griffin presents his proposal to his friend George Levitan, editor of *Sepia,* both Levitan and his editorial director, Mrs. Jackson, warn him of the risks involved. Essentially, two kinds of hostile reactions are defined by their arguments. First, there is the danger of reaction from hate groups who feel free to take the law into their own hands at any time to make an example of a person who would violate established taboos or threaten to change in any way the pattern of their lives or their carefully nurtured ignorance and prejudice. It is such people who were responsible for the notorious Mack Parker lynching mentioned later in the book and who, historically, have been the mainstay of vigilante groups like the Ku Klux Klan and various White Citizens Councils. In these and similar groups, those whom Levitan calls the "ignorant rabble" are manipulated by a few "civic leaders" of the type Griffin later encounters in the Alabama grandfather who gives him a ride through the swamp country. Such a man has been conditioned by his whole upbringing to believe in *our* race," "*our* way of life," and to consider all who endanger the "purity" of either as enemies or defilers.

The second kind of hostility is less violent but no less malicious: it would involve complete social rejection for Griffin and his family. This rejection might come from people with various motives — those who would feel repulsion at the very idea of a white man assuming a non-white identity; those who would resent any action which might "stir up trouble"; and, saddest of all, those "decent" whites who would be prevented by fear from showing courtesy to a man who violated the taboos of their society. Because all these reactions are not merely possible but realistically likely to occur, Griffin feels that he must secure his wife's approval for his project.

Despite the risks, she agrees; and Griffin, his decision now firm, returns to the barn he uses as an office. Here, he soon becomes preoccupied with the sounds and smells and general atmosphere of an autumn night. Significantly, it is the sense of loneliness and fear which the night conveys to him that dominates his mood at the end of this day of decision. The Negro poet Langston Hughes had allied the night with the condition of the black man in the lines from which Griffin took the title of his book: ". . . Night coming tenderly/ Black like me." Night is both tender and hostile for the black man. On the one hand, it masks the poverty of his surroundings, shields him from the hate-filled stares of whites, and affirms his validity and beauty by showing him that blackness is part of the pattern of nature. On the other, its quietness and darkness emphasize his loneliness, isolation, and even fear, in a white-dominated society. Griffin's reactions now are of the second sort; they seem to be a foretaste of his despair in the Hattiesburg hotel room and of his lonely night at the shack in the Alabama swamps.

Closely allied to his fear of isolation is the fear of losing his identity. Once he is black, will whites treat him as a person, as John Howard Griffin, or simply as a nameless Negro? But he already knows the answer: in their minds, his blackness will be like the night, blurring their ability to see him as an individual and alienating him from the world's light and happiness, which these whites claim as their exclusive right.

The first six days of November are involved with the final preparations for entry into black society—the changing of Griffin's skin color and the choice of a suitable contact to make the transition smoother. Before and during the dermatologist's treatments to darken his skin, Griffin wanders the streets of the French Quarter of New Orleans as a white man. His thoughts move backward to the days when he was blind and could only smell and hear and taste the varying delights of the bustling streets and gracious old-world surroundings. His sight is now restored and he contrasts the present with the past experience. But his thoughts also move forward to an anticipated contrast; in one sense, his present vision is still limited—he cannot really see New Orleans yet with the eyes of a black man. The gourmet delights of elegant restaurants which he can now freely enjoy will be barred to him as a Negro. How many other more basic pleasures, how many actual needs, will also be denied to him?

During this period of transition, Griffin finds his conversations with the dermatologist disturbing. The doctor is the first of a number of reasonably well-intentioned whites the journalist encounters who cannot rise above certain widely propagated myths about blacks. Light-skinned Negroes, he tells Griffin, are more trustworthy than the darker ones. Griffin is astonished and alarmed that an educated man could accept such a notion; it seems to the journalist that such falsehoods are invented by those who wish to divide Negroes into factions, and to lessen their chances for progress by fostering a kind of internal racism whereby a lighter Negro would learn to despise a darker one, regarding him as inferior. The doctor also seems to see blacks as naturally violent people and tells Griffin that they have a destructive attitude toward members of their own race. But while the doctor's observations of knife fights among blacks in New Orleans' ghettos are undoubtedly not just inventions on his part, he nevertheless has not stopped to consider that such eruptions of violence may be the products not of inborn tendencies in the race, but of the white man's denial to Negroes of all legitimate opportunities for a decent standard of living, for education, for personal advancement, and for self-expression.

The final step in Griffin's preparation is the finding of a contact for entry into the black community. His choice is Sterling Williams, a man whose life shows some of the severe limitations imposed on blacks in the South. He is an elderly shoeshine "boy" — a man of considerable intelligence and personal strength who is relegated by white society to servitude in menial tasks. To white racists, Williams is a perpetual "boy," not because of any deficiencies in his natural talents but because of the whites' inability to regard blacks as fully mature human beings, commanding the same respect they do. At worst, a black man is viewed as an animal; at best, as a child, regardless of his age or intelligence. Ironically, Williams lost a leg in World War I, defending this very society which represses him.

With the choice of a contact, the period of decisions, plans, and preparations comes to an end. It is time for Griffin to assume his new identity.

PART II: TRANSFORMATION AND FIRST EXPERIENCES AS A BLACK MAN (NEW ORLEANS; NOVEMBER 7-14)

On the night of November 7, John Howard Griffin takes the final steps to transform himself into a black man: after he shaves his head and heightens the tone of his already darkened skin with a stain, he looks into the mirror and sees the new self he has produced. He is overwhelmed with panic and a sense of acute isolation. What was intended as merely a superficial visual change has made him unrecognizable even to himself. All his inclinations rebel: if his children and his friends saw him now, they would see only a large bald Negro, no one that they knew.

This painful crisis of identity is, however, much more than a simple outpouring of Griffin's personal anguish and confusion. For one thing, it marks his first gut realization of the anonymity of the black man to whites. And it also reveals that even a dedicated crusader for human rights, one whose sense of outrage and compassion were sufficient to bring him to this dramatic step, even such a man cannot easily free his deepest emotional reactions from the conditioning of an essentially racist society.

Griffin says that his immense feeling of loneliness was not because he was suddenly a Negro, but because the man he had been, the self he knew, was "hidden in the flesh of another." A few paragraphs later, he tells us that he felt no kinship with the person he saw in the mirror. Griffin is more than lonely; he feels a loss of who he is, and he even feels momentarily repulsed by the new person he appears to have become. The cause of these feelings of alienation and isolation are surely rooted in the racism of his society. For, if such racism did not exist, the step Griffin is taking would not be such a drastic one: if white men did not so despise and repress blacks, changing the color of one's skin would not be a cause for rejection by friends or deprivation of human rights. Furthermore, Griffin himself, although he emphatically repudiates this racism, has been reared and has lived much of his life in a society dominated by it. Thus, while Griffin is no bigot or hypocrite, it should not be too surprising that his emotions may not perfectly conform to his ideals in a situation like the present one. In fact, his relatively progressive thinking on the issue of racial justice may have actually reinforced any remaining, unconsciously negative reactions to blackness. On the one hand, his conventional Southern upbringing taught him about the absolute inferiority of Negroes; later, his more detached observations convinced him that Negroes were the victims of incredible repression, that it was tragic to be born a black man in American society, especially in the South. Thus Griffin is probably unable, on an emotional level, to picture life as a Negro as anything but desolate or hopeless. His negativity toward blackness is evident when Griffin remarks, as he sees his new black self in the mirror, that his "reflections led back to Africa, back to the shanty and the ghetto, back to the fruitless struggles against the mark of blackness."

While Griffin will in certain ways come to identify himself as black rather than white, his comprehension of his new identity will necessarily be limited, especially at first. And at this point, the main way in which he tries to identify himself as a Negro is through beginning to see himself as black enough and ugly enough (in the eyes of whites) to be discriminated against, hated, and oppressed.

As Griffin prepares to venture forth for the first time as a black man, his sense of loneliness and the loss of his familiar identify increases. In fact, the situation begins to take on a certain mysterious, even eerie, quality which detaches it from the comforting familiarity of everyday life. For one thing, as we have already seen, Griffin regards the total effect of his physical transformation as something out of the ordinary; he fears that he has unknowingly "tampered with the mystery of existence" in some way, for his preparations have resulted not in a simple disguise but in a kind of rebirth into a totally new identity. Moreover, his sense of strangeness is reinforced when he answers a phone call for his absent host and realizes that the person at the other end of the line cannot know that he is talking to a Negro.

The timing of this unusual scene also deserves our attention. Griffin, having perfected his physical disguise, hears the clock strike midnight and remarks that it is "time to go." His words imply that this hour is either a necessary or an appropriate time for his departure. We do know, of course, that he wishes to leave the house before his host returns, in order to conceal the nature of the project from him. But is it simply coincidence that both a new day and what Griffin has called his "new life" begin simultaneously? Or did his novelist's attention to symbolic details lead him consciously or unconsciously to choose this specific time? Still another aspect of the midnight hour seems uncannily appropriate: as we may recall from our childhood fairy tales, it is the legendary hour of mysterious transformations of identity and of encounters with the supernatural.

We cannot know with certainty which of these implications Griffin intended that we should draw from the scene. But one thing is evident: the mood and details of his narrative make it clear that the step he is taking is far more than a reporter's clever gimmick to get a good story. Rather, this moment of transformation has touched the deepest recesses of Griffin's consciousness and will profoundly affect his view of himself and of others.

Griffin steps forth from his friend's house a black man in appearance. His description of his first impressions continues the sense of beginning a new life; he reacts initially as would a very young child, discovering new details about his environment, the people around him, and himself. For instance, he notices that his sweat feels the same as when he was white. Nor are the familiar smells of the streets and shops any different to the Negro Griffin. Like a child, he finds that he must learn the proper behavior for each new situation: he must, for example, remember to let a white man on the streetcar first and must remember to seat himself in the rear of the bus. Ironically, these demeaning actions constitute his first "successes" in playing the role of a black man.

One discovery is both comforting and disturbing: other people's complete acceptance of him as black. On the one hand, Griffin is reassured to find that he can pass among Negroes as one of them; there is no suspicion in their behavior toward him, no hesitation in recommending a Negro hotel to him. On the other hand, the journalist has his first direct experience of a phenomenon any black man has to recognize as a condition of his existence in a racist society—invisibility. Griffin walks by the same amusement places he passed as a white man several days earlier and he buys cigarettes at the drugstore he usually patronizes. But as a black man he is no longer an individual, an identity, a person to whites; the formerly insistent hawkers for the girlie shows simply do not see him now, and the woman at the drugstore, though willing to take his money, recognizes him only as a "sale," not as a person, not like the white Griffin with whom she regularly paused to exchange friendly remarks.

Griffin here is undergoing an experience so basic to men born black in this society that it is a common theme in black literature — for instance, Ralph Ellison's famous novel, *Invisible Man*. To most whites, no black man is recognized or acknowledged as an individual; he is simply one of "them." And "they," by many whites' common unspoken assent, are treated according to the principle that, if you refuse to acknowledge something for long enough, it may simply cease to exist. This procedure, despite its logical unsoundness, has become so much a part of various institutions in the South that, as Griffin's later experiences prove, the black man in effect does not exist as a political, economic, or social entity in many areas.

Griffin's first night as a black man ends in a drab room in the town's best Negro hotel. Significantly, he made no arrangement prior to his transformation for a place to sleep. In Southern society, it would be unheard of for a white man to go into a Negro section of town to locate a hotel room for a black. Whites would be shocked to find one of their race doing a favor for a Negro or regarding him as a friend; likewise, Negroes would be understandably suspicious of a white man's motives.

But his reception as a black man among other Negroes is easy and natural. In this hotel, he encounters for the first time the incredible courtesy and friendliness to strangers that he is to find characteristic of most blacks he meets. The unassuming kindness of the man in the shower room alleviates Griffin's loneliness and temporarily insulates him from the hostility and coldness of the outside world. In narrating this episode, Griffin for the first time expresses some emotional acceptance of himself as black by speaking of himself and other Negroes as "us" and by describing the heartening effect of contact with "others like me."

On the following day, November 8, Griffin's black identity is more fully accepted by others and understood by himself. A crucial test of his self-confidence and of the plausibility of his actions in his new role is how Sterling Williams, the shoeshine man who knew the journalist as a white, will react. But there is really no problem; once Sterling has overcome his initial amazement at Griffin's transformation, he gradually lapses into the familiarity of one black man to another. Griffin, caught up as Sterling is by the illusion, begins to show in his language not only the inclusion of himself when he speaks of "we Negroes" but also the separation of himself from "the white man." Moreover, while he is talking with Sterling, the mood lightens when an attractive Negro widow makes a dignified but obvious play for Griffin.

Having been relieved, therefore, of much of his self-consciousness, Griffin is able to join with Sterling and with Joe, Williams' partner, in their day's activities. And it is through the relationships that develop over their lunch that Griffin begins to get a less superficial notion of some of the values which are held by the Negroes he encounters. We should recall that Griffin as a white man had evidently taken delight in gourmet food—as his recollections of the French Quarter revealed. And when he had eaten his first meal as a black man in a small cafe near his hotel, he had remarked on the absence of butter and a napkin. Here with Sterling and Joe, Griffin learns to readjust his values. The important things for him as a black man are, in the first place, simply to have *enough* food and to establish a feeling of brotherhood with others during the meal, some sense of sharing and belonging. Niceties and refinements are unimportant: this meal is basically a kind of coon and rice mixture, cooked in a gallon can on the sidewalk and served in cut-down milk cartons. But it is satisfying and it establishes among the three a feeling of community. Furthermore, partly because of their ability not only to provide adequately for themselves but also to share what they have, Joe and Sterling have a sense of dignity which elevates them far above the status of the wino nearby. Griffin enters into the spirit of the occasion and shares the delight and the self-respect gained from first observing the beggar's misery compared to their own well being, and later relieving that misery by giving him their scraps. The scene foreshadows the one much later in the narrative when Griffin eats an even poorer meal with the family in the Alabama swamps and again perceives the importance of brotherhood and sharing as associated with eating.

But the majority of Griffin's experiences on this day are not nearly so pleasant as this meal. He awakens to the sounds and images of the ghetto, and as he walks through the streets, he views it for the first time from the perspective of someone who belongs there. He can no longer feel the detached pity of the outside observer; he now shares the overwhelming despair that pervades the district and he feels the powerful appeal of any means of escape. But the means are pitifully limited. One man tells Griffin he often rides a bus to a white section of town so he can at least *look* at houses where people are able to live in decent conditions. Others turn to drink or to any other form of pleasure which can provide a temporary distraction from the hopelessness of their lives.

As the day progresses, Griffin's conversations with blacks and his encounters with whites form a kind of initiation to the indignities and forms of repression a black man must suffer. Perhaps one of the most incredible discoveries Griffin makes is that there seems to be a conspiracy to prevent Negroes from satisfying their most basic needs. A black man, Griffin learns, had better locate the few rest rooms and drinking fountains he is permitted to use and stick close to them or he may have to walk miles to find either. To his astonishment, even the most decrepit skid row toilets are carefully segregated. Another apparently systematic means of oppression is revealed to Griffin in a conversation at the YMCA Coffee Shop. As the cafe owner explains, whites single out the light-skinned, better looking, and more stylishly dressed Negroes and try to divide the race by creating in them a condescending attitude toward the darker Uncle Toms.

In some ways, though, the hardest thing for Griffin to endure as a one-day-old black man is the term "nigger." The word seems to leap out at him from otherwise unintelligible conversations, concrete evidence of the stupid and senseless hatred constantly directed toward Negroes. By the end of the day, even the church bell seems to him to clang out the word "nigger" and a series of prohibitions with it: you can't go in there; you can't drink here; we don't serve niggers."

The culmination of Griffin's encounters with white hostility is the episode when a young white bully threateningly pursues him along a series of lonely streets. The incident is dramatic evidence that the black man is being perpetually sought out by forces of hatred just as irrational and unprovoked as this boy's aggression. After Griffin finally escapes to the steps of a church, the boy's insults continue to ring through his brain, alternating with the word "nigger." It is only then that the journalist seems to realize that none of the names the bully called him — "Baldy," "Mr. No-Hair," Mr. Shithead" — was a racist epithet. Yet the journalist wonders if it would have happened if he were white. He will never know, of course, but he has strong reason to suspect that it would not.

In the midst of the day's insults and terrors, Griffin finds occasions which teach him something about what his self-concept as a black man ought to include. The key words among most New Orleans Negroes seem to be *unity* and *dignity*. Both words take on new meaning for Griffin during the morning's incident on the bus. Griffin takes a seat which is on the dividing line between black and white sections. As the bus starts to fill up, whites choose to stand rather than take vacant seats in the Negro section. When Griffin starts to offer his seat to a tired-looking white woman, the frowns of nearby Negroes deter him from "going against the race." For if blacks are unified in their refusal to yield the seats they are allowed by custom to occupy, whites may eventually feel uncomfortable enough to sit beside them; a victory will have been won. Thus, the blacks on the bus are making their sense of brotherhood effective. This quiet unity will be the basis for even more effective unity in their later struggle against whites.

The question of dignity is also involved. As the cafe owner at the Y later explains to Griffin, black people have too often been humiliated into doing anything to please whites (for example, giving them their seats on buses) and have thus failed to advance their own race and their own dignity in the eyes of whites. Sterling Williams also voices concern about black dignity; the best way to avoid trouble with whites, he tells Griffin, is to mind your own business and be polite, but *not* to bow and scrape. "Show you got some dignity," he urges.

In short, many New Orleans Negro leaders urge their followers to adopt a policy of using courtesy to shame the white man into acknowledging and yielding his rights. Such a plan is summed up in the poster Griffin sees on the wall of a restaurant; it details a method to desegregate buses by emphasizing prayer, politeness, neatness, avoiding arguments, and believing in the ultimate power of good to dominate evil. Such a philosophy, of course, was the foundation of the Southern civil rights movement and was most prominent in the leadership of Martin Luther King, Jr. Tragically, the assassination of King seemed rather to affirm the power of evil over good.

The rest of Griffin's days in New Orleans (November 10-14) are filled with the same basic contrasts which characterized the first: on the one hand, the kindness of most Negroes to him and their dignified efforts to lead decent lives; on the other, the whites' systematic tactics to prevent black advancement and their spontaneous displays of hatred.

In the first instance, Griffin many times experiences the courtesy and quiet dignity of the city's blacks. For example, there is the college student he meets who walks several miles out of his way to show the journalist, a complete stranger, how to get to a movie theater. And there are also the continually impressive and enlightening conversations Griffin has with the black businessmen and civic leaders at the Y cafe. In these conversations, he learns more about further white tactics of oppression, especially what the cafe owner terms economic injustice. As he explains, whites try to frustrate black advancement by refusing to hire even the best educated and most highly qualified Negroes. Only postal jobs, preaching, and teaching positions are available — and very few of these. Such limitations not only severely curtail black earning power but also make it impossible for blacks to pay very much in taxes. Whites then argue that, since Negroes contribute so little to the support of the government, their rights do not deserve the same consideration as those of white people. And the race issue is made even more complicated, the proprietor and Mr. Gayle explain, by whites' insinuations that any move toward economic equality or racial justice is either anti-Christian or anti-American.

Finally, Griffin also encounters further instances of spontaneous, personal discrimination or malice. In one case, the rebuff is delivered with such a show of courtesy that he does not realize until later that the man asking him to leave a bench in a public park was not doing him a favor by warning him of a place Negroes could not sit, but was personally denying him the right to occupy a bench which blacks were customarily allowed to use. A second incident recalls the more overt hatred of the white bully, though it is more inventive in its malice. In this case, a driver on the bus back from Dillard University plays a cat-and-mouse game with the exhausted journalist, slamming the door in his face just as he wants to get off, and forcing him to ride eight blocks past his stop. While Griffin remarks that this kind of behavior was not typical of the city's bus drivers, he and his readers are beginning to realize that racism in some form *is* typical of the whites he meets and that similar overt displays of hatred are, unfortunately, far from uncommon.

Such, then, are Griffin's experiences in New Orleans, the first place he comes to know from the perspective of a black man. On November 14, as he prepares to leave for Mississippi, he sifts through his impressions of the city. Griffin's first week as a Southern black man began in personal confusion and fear. His early experiences were understandably shocking and depressing, but he found some comfort in the dignified persistence of the blacks he met and signs of hope in the apparent courtesy of many whites. As the week drew to a close, however, the cumulative effect of his encounters with institutionalized injustice and personal malice has made him more embittered and pessimistic.

In such a mood, Griffin pauses to evaluate the attitudes of New Orleans whites. Initially, the journalist had been impressed by the courtesy of whites to blacks in this city; his questions about directions to various places were usually politely answered and his job inquiries politely refused. The Rev. Mr. Davis had confirmed this general impression in one of their conversations at the Y cafe: a New Orleans white, he claimed, could be courteous to a black man without fear of being called a "nigger lover," as in other places in the South.

But as Griffin leaves the city, he voices his disillusionment with the so-called graciousness of its whites. This politeness, he concludes, is only a thin veneer designed to cover up the basic fact that the black in New Orleans is still a tenth-class citizen, assaulted by racist epithets, and barred from eating, drinking, and using a toilet in the same places as white men—as though his actual bodily functions were of a lower order.

At this point, Griffin also sets down his observations on one very important fact: all rebuffs against a man because of his color —no matter how universally applied to his race, no matter how institutionalized—are always felt and experienced as personal insults, personal wounds. If you are barred from eating at a lunch counter, it is no comfort to know that it is because of your race rather than because of your personality. The basic premise underlying all such prohibitions, the journalist points out, is the racist's refusal to see any black as an individual, distinct from the mass of the Negro race. And while the white man consistently asserts his own individuality and denies that blacks can generalize about whites, he essentially sees all Negroes as alike and believes that they are, as a race, inferior to his own. Moreover, he has arranged things to bear out his prejudices: having deprived blacks of economic and political influence; of decent housing, education, and jobs; of most basic rights, including the right to exist as an individual, the white racist then points to many Negroes' lack of self-esteem, to the high incidence of drunkenness and dope addiction, to the squalid living conditions of the ghettos, as proof that black men are essentially lower by nature than white men.

In Griffin's final evaluation, then, there is in New Orleans some attempt to mask with superficial courtesies the presence of institutionalized policies of racism that control and exploit blacks economically and politically. Overt malice is not characteristic of the city's whites, but it is common enough to be shocking. All this is bad enough. But what is it like in Mississippi and Alabama, where there is no urbane, old-world charm to veil the concentrated efforts to destroy a race, and where personal expressions of hatred are reinforced by general approval? It is time, Griffin decides, for him to find out.

A strong indication of what it is like, in Mississippi at least, is provided by the news which Sterling reports to Griffin that morning—the failure of the Pearl River County Grand Jury to return any indictments against those involved in the lynching of Mack Parker.

The Parker case did not attract only local attention; it was a matter of national interest for nearly a year and spurred on attempts by liberal United States senators and congressmen to strengthen existing civil rights legislation. The details of the case make it an almost perfect example of what Sterling contemptuously calls "southern justice." Parker, a twenty-three-year-old Negro truck driver, was in the Poplarville, Mississippi, jail awaiting trial for the alleged rape of a white woman. On the night of April 25, 1959, according to the reports of other prisoners, nine or ten masked or hooded white men entered the unguarded jail, located the cell key, beat up Parker's cellmate, C. J. Monday, and pulled the struggling Parker out. Monday stated that Parker kept yelling "Help, I didn't do it."

The prisoners' accounts also bear out the details Bill Williams gives Griffin as they pass through Poplarville on the bus to Hattiesburg. The lynchers dragged Parker down the stairs from his third floor cell, his head bouncing off each metal tread on the way. A trail of blood on the stairs and bloody hand prints on the walls attested to the brutality of his treatment.

National reaction to the incident was swift; a special squad of FBI agents was immediately dispatched to investigate. On May 5, Parker's body was found, and the following day a coroner's jury ruled that his death was due to bullet wounds. At this point, however, the Southern process of justice took over. Although the FBI had submitted to Mississippi authorities a 378-page report which supposedly identified members of the mob and included admissions of guilt from some, the Pearl River County Grand Jury completely ignored the report. On November 5, the jury adjourned without returning any indictments. The news of this adjournment, which evidently reached the New Orleans Negro community about a week later, deepened their despair over "white man's justice."

In later developments, a federal grand jury was set up to investigate the case, but in order to indict, it was necessary for them to conclude that a violation of federal kidnapping or civil rights laws had been involved. On January 15, 1960, a jury of twenty whites and one Negro announced that it had found no basis for federal prosecution. In other words, the state, under whose jurisdiction the case legally fell, had carried out its technical, if not its moral, responsibilities; existing federal laws, in the jury's opinion, did not provide a basis for prosecution. The hands of justice were tied.

In order to understand the impact of the Parker case upon Southern blacks, we must recognize what attitudes and tendencies it seemed to represent. First of all, there was the whites' tolerance of vigilante violence. The *New York Times* reported that, while it appeared that most Southern whites disapproved of depriving any man of a "fair trial," there was still in some parts of the Deep South—especially in the rural areas—secret or open approval of mob action, particularly in the case of an alleged sex crime by a black. Second, there was the constant perversion of justice in cases involving Negroes. It was highly unlikely that Parker or any other black man could have received a fair trail in Mississippi, since blacks were systematically excluded from serving on local juries. (The Supreme Court, in fact, had previously reversed a conviction of a Negro in that state on these grounds.) As further evidence of legal bias, Poplarville residents told reporters that they supported the Pearl River County jury's failure to indict the lynchers because no local jury would have convicted them anyway. Therefore, although the incidence of actual lynchings had diminished in the 1950s, other means of depriving blacks of their legal rights and the failure to prosecute crimes against blacks were still typical in the Deep South.

Thus, it is the news of the Parker case which makes Griffin decide to go into Mississippi, despite Sterling's warning, "That's no place for a colored man." Griffin believes that he must have firsthand knowledge of Mississippi as a black man in order to disprove its white leaders' contentions that relationships between the races are harmonious and that outsiders "just don't understand" about things like lynchings.

As we have seen, then, there seems to be a kind of "if you think New Orleans is bad, you should see Mississippi and Alabama" idea running through Griffin's mind as he prepares for his departure. Ironically, just as he is leaving, circumstances seem to conspire to show him how bad New Orleans really is. First he encounters blatant discrimination when stores he regularly patronized as a black refuse to cash a traveler's check, a service afforded to white men without question. Griffin's reaction here proves a point he made earlier: it is impossible not to feel such rebuffs as personal insults; each refusal seems to imply that Griffin probably stole the checks.

The journalist's next unpleasant experience involves the ticket seller at the bus station. She, like the teenage bully or the driver on the bus from Dillard, simply pours out upon Griffin undeserved malice and hatred. Her refusal at first to change a ten-dollar bill is accompanied by what blacks term a "hate stare," an unbelievably exaggerated expression of loathing and contempt. A white man in the bus station also fixes the journalist with such a look. But whatever fears Griffin might have felt are completely overcome by his utter horror at the fact that any human being could be so consumed with such inhuman and obscene passion. Nevertheless, the horror of these people's behavior does not deprive Griffin of his own human compassion. He is able to see the two whites as victims of those emotional reactions which they have been encouraged by society to cultivate, for he speaks of the woman as "possessed" by her fury, and he pities the man for destroying his own humanity by the passions which have made him their prey.

The ironies of this situation are many, and Griffin does not allow them to escape his readers. Like most ironies, they are based on certain contrasts between the apparent and the actual, or between limited knowledge and fuller perception. The two whites' feelings of superiority to the black man they see before them are obvious: they believe they are acting in such a way as to show clearly what outstanding people they are by emphatically disapproving of a man who represents a race and a social class which their society has little regard for. This is the "truth" as it is apparent to them. But Griffin's horror and, above all, his pity show us what these whites really are — people without a true sense of their own worth, who must put up a show of self-esteem by finding others whom they can classify as "inferior." If they cannot say with confidence, I am just, I am honest, I am compassionate, I am generous, at least they can say I am not poor, I am not shabby, I am not black. The tragic irony of their attempt to elevate their own standing in this way is pointed up by Griffin's silent cry to the man in the station: what in God's name are you doing to yourself? For Griffin has seen — and has let us see — that this man does not have enough self-respect to recognize that whatever humanity he does possess is completely negated by the gross inhumanity of his present attitude. Both he and the woman are engaged in a kind of moral and emotional self-mutilation without realizing it.

A final instance of irony arises after the journalist has retired to the Negroes' waiting room in the station. Here, he picks up one of the books he has recently purchased and it falls open to a statement by Plato. According to Plato, the essence of a man's humanity is his ability to act in a just way. What notion could provide a greater contrast to the behavior Griffin has just witnessed?

Griffin's reflections on his stay in New Orleans, the news about the Parker case, and now the episode in the bus station have formed an ominous prelude to his bus ride into Mississippi. Unfortunately the omens will prove to have been accurate, for it is at the end of this day that Griffin will find his despair almost unbearable. In a more immediate incident, Griffin, having just witnessed what he called insanity in the behavior of the two whites, encounters on the bus an equally unbalanced black man, the handsome, frustrated Christophe.

Christophe is one of the most vivid and complex characters Griffin encounters. Basic to his personality, as it was to that of the two whites in the station, is a lack of self-esteem. But in the Negro's case, his lack of a sense of worth is undoubtedly directly connected with the penalties society imposes on him because of his race. Christophe is exactly the kind of person who would suffer most acutely from such societal limitations; he is sensitive, extraordinarily intelligent, handsome, and a man of obvious ability. But for the Southern black, the opportunities for achievement, as we have seen from Griffin's fruitless job inquiries and from the conversations in the Y cafe, are almost nonexistent.

So Christophe, who might have learned several languages well, who might have been a scholar or a diplomat, now can only throw out fragments of various tongues in a snobbish, and at the same time pitiable, play for recognition. This handsome, elegant young man, who might have been a movie or stage star had he been white, has learned to so despise the "Negro-ness" which prevents such success that he hates all that seems to him characteristic of "damned punk niggers"; thus he tries to cultivate those modes of dress, speech, and behavior which he hopes will gain him favor among whites. In fact, Christophe has been so thoroughly victimized by the distorted values of a racist society that he acts very similar to the two whites in the bus station: in order to convince himself of his own worth he must find a group he believes he can classify as inferior to himself and make it the object of his contempt. Tragically, the group is his own race. Christophe ends up in the hopeless dilemma of a man who hates the group with which society identifies him, yet who is unable to pass into the group whose approval he seeks.

The consequences of this dilemma and of the frustrations which Christophe must have encountered again and again in his desire for achievement and recognition are all too obvious. His behavior to the other blacks on the bus is contemptuous, quarrelsome, and potentially violent. And, as Griffin soon learns, he has turned to a life of crime, probably as the only way to achieve a sense of distinction and importance in relation to other men. The tragedy of this ultimate perversion of Christophe's talents is dramatized by the fact that his revelation of his plans to "shoot up a couple of guys" comes immediately after his tearful request to be remembered in the prayers of Griffin, whom he takes to be a priest. Even from a totally secular perspective, Christophe is a "lost soul," for he has long ago forsaken all that could legitimately fulfill his sense of selfhood—and he is too deeply entrenched in illegitimate fulfillment ever to retrace his steps. When Christophe gets off the bus, he leaves Griffin feeling both relieved and compassionate.

Fortunately, Griffin's further conversations with blacks on the bus are of an entirely different sort. As a matter of fact, he begins to notice that the Negroes who board the bus in the little towns in Mississippi seem to make special efforts to be warm and friendly to the other blacks—as if they feel the need to protect each other against the hostility of the whites. One young man, Bill Williams, is especially helpful to Griffin. Bill and several other Negro passengers try to give the new visitor to the state a number of hints about how to avoid trouble, including never looking at a white woman—or even a picture of one—and expecting trouble at any time.

But if the companionship among the blacks on the bus is comforting, there are still reminders of what if will be like when they get off. The bus driver's refusal to let the blacks off for a rest stop exemplifies the same tactic of oppression by inconvenience which Griffin discovered in New Orleans. And the passage through Poplarville, the scene of the Mack Parker lynching, is a grim foretaste of the degree to which repression is allowed to go in the deepest parts of the South. Bill Williams describes some of the details of the mob's brutality and points out the courthouse where the decision was made not to bring the lynchers to trial.

Had it not been for the description of the Poplarville mob, the procedure Bill sets up to get Griffin a safe room in Hattiesburg would appear outlandish. But tactics which would seem like clock-and-dagger maneuvers in another setting are absolutely necessary here, as is proven by Griffin's encounter with a carload of angry whites and by the stories his second contact tells him.

Safe at last in a decrepit room, Griffin is oppressed by his thoughts. Someone in the tavern below sings of "poor Mack Parker," and the sadness and senselessness of it all overwhelms the journalist. When he stares into the cracked mirror and sees himself crying, we are reminded of the first night of his transformation into a black man. But his present reactions, in one sense, contrast strongly with his past ones. Now, far from rebelling against his black identity, he feels so utterly engulfed by it that he is momentarily overcome by a surge of blind hatred against the whites who force black men like himself into what he describes as a hell of loneliness, despair, and alienation. But his hatred soon gives way to grief as he ponders the sickness that could motivate whites, "my own people," to such injustice against their fellow human beings.

What Griffin feels at this moment is more than personal; it is part of the same pattern of hopelessness which led Christophe to his self-destructive behavior. And Griffin, looking around the room, finds evidence that one of its previous tenants shared his despair. The blank film negatives call up in his mind an image of some past inhabitant returning to the room with his package of photos, but finding instead of familiar faces only blank nothingness. Whether or not the negatives had ever been involved in

such an episode, Griffin uses them here to project for us a striking image of his frustration and that of all black men. For Griffin
too is seeking a familiar source of comfort when he tries to write
to his wife; but the page of his notebook, like the negatives, re-
mains blank.

The main barrier to the "black" Griffin's communication
with his white wife is a deeply engrained Southern attitude about
race and sex. Racists have long preached the concept of Negro
inferiority, insisting that blacks are basically more animalistic
than whites. In order to insure that the "inferior" race will be
kept in its place, these whites have linked up racial attitudes
with one of the most basic human fears – the fear of sexual violation. Thus most Southern white women have been directly or
indirectly encouraged to believe that Negro men, portrayed as
more sensual in nature than whites, and as endowed with larger
or more potent sex organs, are constantly lusting for relationships
with the "superior" white woman and are ready to take her by
force if the opportunity arises. As a consequence, black men in
the South have been rebuked and, in some cases, beaten or arrested for literally *looking* at a white woman. (As we will see
later in the narrative, the Southern attitude toward the relationship between a white man and a black woman is an entirely dif-
erent matter.)

Griffin has long been conscious of these racial-sexual fears
and of the myth of the Negro's "rape impulse." His journals
reveal that when he was first considering this project he feared
that his becoming a black man might cause his wife some hesitation about resuming normal relations with him when he returned.
(Fortunately, his fears proved to be groundless.) Already, Griffin
in his black identity has been constantly reminded to keep "in
his place," as far as white women are concerned. We recall, for
instance, the remarks of the tired white woman on the New
Orleans bus – to whom Griffin almost gave his seat; we also recall
the warnings Bill Williams gave Griffin about how to behave in
Mississippi. But the journalist never quite imagined that his own
reactions would be so inhibited by these attitudes as they are
now. For he finds that he, as a Negro, cannot be so bold as to
write "Darling" to a white woman.

The insistent rhythm of the juke box below reminds Griffin of another stereotype somewhat allied to the myth of Negro sensuality—the white man's concept of the "happy darky." There are two aspects to this notion. On the one hand, whites conjure up pictures of childlike Negroes, free of worries and eagerly awaiting the opportunity to show their gratitude by singing and dancing for the white folks who take care of them. This image, a relic of slave days, may comfort the whites who see "the good old days" as a model of the way the two races ought to be related, but it always had one overwhelming fault in the eyes of black men: it was a lie. It denied them the fundamental role of adults, the right to free themselves from paternal care, to act in their own interests, to please themselves first. And so, Griffin bitterly reflects, they finally escaped from the oppression of slavery and paternalism to the "freedom" of ghettos and shanty towns. But the "happy darky" myth followed them, taking on a second form. In this new aspect, whites see the blaring juke boxes, the frequent drunkenness, and the apparent sensuality of the ghettos as evidence that Negroes are happy amid squalid surroundings. The black man, supposedly lacking higher sensibilities and finer feelings, is seen by them as content to live in such subhuman conditions because "he doesn't know any better."

Griffin reflects on both aspects of the myth with intense bitterness. Every feature of his surroundings, every facet of his present emotions dramatically refutes the idea that Negroes have some innate ability to be happy, to rise above the incredible oppression to which they are daily subjected. Gross laughter, loud music, too much food or drink—Griffin sees these not as evidence of "whooping it up" but as frantic attempts to survive by somehow dulling the pain of existence for even a brief time. In this desperate pursuit of pleasure by men who are denied happiness, and in the whites' blatant refusal to acknowledge the blacks' frustration and despair, Griffin also senses a potential for madness, for violence. From the perspective of a decade which has seen Watts and Jackson State, we see that his words were prophetic.

Thus the painfulness of Griffin's thoughts becomes overwhelming. One week of existence as a black man has brought him to the edge of utter despondency, and he decides to escape temporarily into the familiar white world. Is he, therefore, to be criticized because he is unable to bear for more than a week what black men must endure all their lives?

To arrive at an answer, we must examine the situation carefully. First of all, not having been a black man all his life, Griffin is undoubtedly spared the cumulative weight of years of oppression and limitation. We have already seen what can happen to one black man of similar talents and intelligence — Christophe. And it is also true that Griffin, as a temporary black man, always knows he can return to a freer, more comfortable life. But there are mitigating circumstances. Griffin is alone in a strange city, isolated from whites by his blackness and unacquainted with any blacks other than the contacts Bill Williams set up for him. He has spent an exhausting week full of an immense variety of new experiences. Moreover, to the black man's normal anxieties about white hostility are added certain tensions involved in pretending to be black, for instance the fear of discovery, or the fear of angering whites by forgetting to act as if he "knows his place." Finally, if a man is born black and has surmounted the continual hatreds and frustrations which are destroying Christophe, he has developed over a period of time certain means of preserving his sanity in order to live from day to day. Sterling Williams and many of the men at the Y cafe are able, through the amazing strength of character they have slowly and painfully achieved, to cope with despair on a daily basis. There is no way to judge whether Griffin — if he had been born black — would have turned out to be a Christophe or a Reverend Davis. But it is probable that the latter man developed resources which cannot be learned in only a week of being black and which are not now available to Griffin.

So Griffin decides to leave the terrors and suffering of the ghetto for a two-day visit with a newspaperman, P. D. East, whom he has corresponded with.

PART III: THE VISIT WITH P. D. EAST
(HATTIESBURG AND NEW ORLEANS; NOVEMBER 14-16)

Most of the facts about P. D. East are revealed to us as Griffin reads the manuscript of East's autobiography. We note immediately the resemblance to the pattern of Griffin's own life — and we are forewarned of the penalties which will be imposed on Griffin in the future because of his present masquerade. Like East, Griffin had been reared to adopt many Southern white prejudices. In Griffin's case it was his life in France and his observation of Hitler's racism which made him perceive the error of his thinking. East's change of heart came under more difficult circumstances: still living in the South, he had to risk both the hostility of his friends and relatives and the financial failure of his newspaper when he decided to become a spokesman for racial justice. As Griffin reads of the threatening phone calls and anonymous letters which East received, and as he observes the social isolation imposed upon East and his family, he must wonder how much of this will also plague him when his project is made public.

But Griffin comes to know East not only as an inspiring crusader but also as a personal friend. And so the Texan's immense admiration is balanced by affectionate amusement at his friend's foibles. Our first view of East is impressive: his quiet courage in approaching Griffin on the dark Hattiesburg street leaves Griffin speechless. Our admiration increases as we share Griffin's reading of the editor's autobiography. But other episodes reveal the lighter side of East's personality; P. D. is in many ways a "character," with certain eccentricities. His human side is spotlighted in the account of his invitation to lecture at Dillard University. P. D., in refusing Dean Gandy's invitation, was secretly hoping to be coaxed into accepting. When Gandy did not press him further, East's ego was hurt, and it becomes a matter of pride for him to show up at Dillard on that day anyway. This incident reveals an amusing and endearing touch of childishness in East's character; and this egotism is reinforced by his need to be "center stage," as seen in the endless comic monologue he delivers the first day of Griffin's visit.

The dominant feature of East's personality, however, is probably his incredible sense of humor. P. D. seems to have found a way to use irony — rather heavyhanded, at times — both to show his concern over a problem or an injustice and yet to avoid sentimentality or emotionalism. The first example of this sort of humor which Griffin encounters comes not from East himself but from his wife, Billie, who greets Griffin as "Uncle Tom" and who set out black towels and washcloth for their guest. The humor both smoothes over the uneasiness of the journalist's entry into the East household and serves as a sympathetic commentary on the absurdity of having to smuggle a guest into one's own house because of the color of his skin. East's own humor reveals itself later as he and Griffin drive through the Dillard campus. Perhaps fearing that the contrast between its spacious lawns and the harsh world which denies educated black men any opportunities to use their training might be too much for his friend, East lightens the mood by parodying typical Southern white bigotry. Moreover, by choosing to satirize precisely those whose policies could make the efforts of the university fruitless, P. D. implies his understanding without stating it overtly. And with his later parody of the racist to Gandy, East is able to say something he could never say straightforwardly without sounding pompous or embarrassing them both: I apologize for the insanity of most of my race and I want you to know that I regard you in every way as an equal and a friend.

On a more profound level, humor is a way for East to cope with tragedy and hardship. When Griffin reads of the terrorism and economic failure which resulted from East's adoption of a "fair" editorial policy in his paper, he sits on his bed and weeps for his friend's misfortune. Yet East wrote some of his most brilliant satires during this period, columns which parodied the very Southern racists who were ruining his social and financial standing. Later on, East shows Griffin documents of Southern injustice which he humorously calls his collection of "assdom." In essence, East, in the midst of personal tragedy and increased awareness of the injustices being done to fellow human beings, was always able to keep a perspective of grim humor which enabled him to retain his mental and emotional balance. The most hopeless situation a man can know is the sense of being completely at the mercy of hostile and malicious forces. But a man who perceives the fundamental absurdity of those who seek to destroy him and who can laugh, however painfully, at it, possesses a power of sorts over his enemies, a security they cannot shake. So it is with East, whose humor is a source of strength and a technique of survival.

But Griffin's visit with East is not only a time of personal contact and comfort; it is also a time for new insights into the problems of the South. Griffin finds that East has long been preoccupied with one particular aspect of Southern policy: the misuse of law to achieve racist goals. East calls it "legalized injustice." There are essentially two categories of misuse: first, the making and enforcement of laws which are fundamentally in violation of the Constitution; and second, the distorted interpretation of valid laws. In the first category, East cited a proposal to use tax funds to support White Citizens Councils, and a bill penalizing churches which held integrated services. In the second category are many of the documents in his "assdom" collection and the outlandish "literacy" tests he jokes about to Dean Gandy. Griffin, along with his friend, reaches the conclusion that it is not only the ranting bigots who are most responsible for continuing repression of these sorts but the shrewd legal minds who deliberately exploit prejudice, fear, and misguided patriotism in order to foster racism.

When Griffin's visit ends, his sense of isolation has been somewhat alleviated. He is comforted to find that another Southern white not only shares his concern about racial injustice but also has had to conquer the resulting loneliness, rejection, and despair. East's experiences indicate to Griffin that his own future may be extremely difficult after his project becomes known; yet East's experiences reassure Griffin that he can find the strength—and the humor—to make it bearable.

PART IV: HITCHHIKING THROUGH MISSISSIPPI AND ALABAMA (BILOXI, MOBILE, MONTGOMERY; NOVEMBER 19-27)

Thematically speaking, this is one of the most unified sections of Griffin's narrative. Although he covers several days of experiences in two states, the journalist describes them to us in such a way as to emphasize the concept of love in its various perverted and ennobling manifestations. Granted that the concept of love, or what Griffin sometimes calls "charity," and its fundamental opposition to all kinds of racism and prejudice, actually runs through many parts of *Black Like Me*, it seems to come into sharpest focus in this section. "Charity," in the sense that Griffin uses the word, means much more than simple philanthropy, the giving of money or goods. It derives from the Latin word *caritas* and means *love*, not in a limited or sexual sense, but in the broadest humanitarian and spiritual applications. In Christian theology, *caritas* is the word used to describe the love which God has for all mankind, the essence of God's being which motivated him to create the universe and man. In this sense the Gospel of John defines the Creator himself: *Deus caritas* — God is love.

In this section, Griffin's treatment of this theme of love will center on certain contrasts: for example, the perverted preoccupations of the drivers who pick him up, as opposed to the selfless marital and familial love of the sawmill worker's household; or the ideals of humanitarian charity and justice, in contrast to the refusal of decent housing, education, and jobs to black people.

The theme of love is first introduced into this section by the pamphlet which Griffin reads as he waits in the New Orleans station for the bus to Biloxi. It suggests to him that "men of good will" can aid the cause of racial justice by trying to rear their children to love and respect all men, whatever their color. This concept of love is a striking contrast to the advertisement for various sexual acts which Griffin reads on the men's room door. In previous sections we have already encountered discussions of the

Southern white myths of the black man's exaggerated sexual drives. Here the stereotype includes black women, whom racists believe to be sensual playthings for white men. Basic to this idea is the notion that Negroes are so lacking in a sense of morality that nothing can insult or debase them. Thus it is not primarily the blatant "sensuality" of these notices that shocks Griffin, but rather the white man's bigoted ignorance of the fact that blacks would find such appeals demeaning. In fact, the most paradoxical aspect of the white man's prejudice is that he can delude himself into feeling vastly superior to "dirty lecherous niggers" while engaging in the grossest exploitation of other human beings in order to satisfy his own lusts.

Griffin's meditation on the men's room notice, however, is not simply moralistic in a generalized way: he treats this incident not just as typical, but as an actual, specific experience involving him and other individuals: the insensitive bigot who put the sign there, and also, most tragically, each poor and desperate soul who may become one of its victims — some man or woman driven by poverty to pimp or to become a prostitute. Griffin's thoughts concentrate on one of the possible victims with whom he can establish a tangible connection — the unknown man who left the part of a loaf of bread Griffin sees on the floor before him. Could he have left the bread uneaten, the journalist asks, because he saw in the notice an opportunity to earn enough for a decent meal, a night's lodging?

Normally a man who would procure "dates" for money would evoke only our contempt. But Griffin here realizes that no man who lives a reasonably comfortable and secure life can know the depths to which he might be driven by privation. Suppose he himself had not been able, the journalist speculates, to cash the traveler's check — and suppose he were not Griffin, the well-to-do white writer, but Griffin, the desperate, unemployed black? Can he say with certainty that he could never be driven by hunger to do what his conscience might condemn? When he reflects that he might have been reduced to the same thing, he imagines a John Howard Griffin with the same talents and intelligence, but born and raised a black man, unable to receive the education or to secure the jobs which could utilize these abilities, and — above all — incapable of rising above the hopeless oppressiveness of his surroundings to develop any idealistic sense of moral behavior. Suppose he was down to his last dime, unable to get a job; suppose he knew a few women who weren't too particular — would he be able to resist the easy money? Griffin's perceptiveness about the relativity of values to one's environment and circumstances stands in direct contrast to the self-righteousness of the bigot.

Most of the whites Griffin meets while hitchhiking illustrate various degrees and types of this hypocrisy. And their hypocrisy generally focuses on the sexual stereotypes already discussed. Griffin says that the drivers seemed to pick him up as they would pick up a book of pornography — they regarded him as an object, an outlet for those desires and curiosities they would consider too shameful to reveal to other whites. However, with a black man they feel no need to keep such urges secret. Griffin's descriptions of these men emphasize the paradoxical and illogical nature of their attitudes: on the one hand, they regard the Negro as so inferior to themselves that they do not need to keep up any show of respectability before him; on the other, their own shamelessness makes their lack of self-respect painfully evident. Like those who give Griffin exaggerated hate stares, the more they make their contempt for others obvious, the more they reveal their contempt for themselves.

But there are also more subtle forms of bigotry. One of the drivers whom Griffin's narrative deals with is an educated young man who puts up a rather pretentious show of scholarly interest in "the Negro." However, he unknowingly reveals that he has a view of blacks which is fundamentally racist, for underlying his statements about Negroes' "healthier attitudes" toward sex is a concept that blacks respond to sex only in a spontaneous, animalistic way, and that they lack any higher sensitivity, any reverence for sexual love as a total commitment of oneself to another. Ironically, this young man shows no evidence in his own remarks and questions that he has anything but a limited view of sexual relationships. He dwells not on marital unions or deep feelings, but on a kind of "free love without guilt" attitude which he supposes to be characteristic of Negroes. The young man seems to be half-admiring and half-contemptuous in his underlying feelings: on the one hand, he would like to be able to engage in unlimited sexual experiences without guilt; on the other, he feels superior to those who he believes lack the "finer morality" which would make them feel guilt and remorse over such casual sex relationships.

The essential error in the young man's thinking is that he has ignored the fact that blacks and whites share a common humanity, a common sense of basic morality; Griffin remarks that the young man sees the Negro "as a different species." The journalist tries to point out to him that any tendency toward more casual sexual attitudes, more explicit gestures or language which whites may believe to be characteristic of blacks, are not racial differences but are determined by the circumstances of their lives. If a man is consistently deprived of every finer pleasure in life — art, literature, music, philosophy — and if he also lacks decent educational opportunities, then sooner or later he may turn to any kind of sensual thrill or crude affection in the vain hope of satisfying his longing for enjoyment, for beauty, for happiness.

The narration of this long conversation between the young man and Griffin is centrally placed in his account of November 19. In fact, the way in which Griffin has chosen to emphasize certain parts of his day's experiences gives an almost symmetrical balance to this unit of his narrative and highlights the various manifestations and distortions of certain kinds of love. The day begins with a local Negro's account of a perversion of humanitarian love: the deliberate "legalized injustice" of using gasoline taxes to support segregated beaches. Next, the kind reasonableness of the young driver from Massachusetts emphasizes by contrast the un-reason and un-love of what is to follow. First, the man who owns the custard stand has long since closed his mind to any appeals for justice toward blacks; he also refuses a direct appeal to his sense of charity when Griffin requests to use a decrepit outhouse. After this second example of the perversion of love in the humanitarian sense, Griffin's narrative turns to the various drivers (including the educated young man described above), whose pornographic curiosity and misguided notions of blacks' sexual practices and attitudes represent a kind of perversion of love in both the sexual and humanitarian senses.

Finally, two encounters, one with a white, the other with a black, balance the hopeful note introduced by the Massachusetts driver and renew Griffin's hopes about the power of love to ennoble the human spirit. The white man is a young construction worker who gives Griffin a lift into Mobile; he seems to be totally "color blind," since he treats the journalist with an ease and a naturalness unique among the Southerners Griffin has met. The only possible source Griffin can discover for the young man's extraordinarily sound attitude is the immensity of the love he feels for his own wife and child—a love which radiates outward to all humanity. If Griffin's hypothesis is correct, this young man is an example, by contrast to the other drivers whom the journalist has met, of the ideal effect of sexual and marital love on the human spirit.

The day's last encounter involves a more ethical and theological notion of love as a moral power to combat injustice and hatred. The old Negro preacher who shares his room with Griffin shows the precise humanitarian tolerance the educated young white driver lacked: he sees even those whites who hate and oppress his people as sharing with him the common bond of being "God's children." And the preacher seems to see the ability to love—in the sense of loving all men, black or white, friend or enemy—as the essence of being human. "When we stop loving them, that's when they win," he states. That is, a man who cannot love is degraded to the lowest level; he is deprived of his humanity.

Perhaps this preacher's insight is, after all, the best summary of the theme of this whole section. For the humanity of each person Griffin meets is in direct proportion to his ability to love, either in the sense of a deep and selfless sexual commitment, or in the sense of a fundamental respect for the dignity of all other human beings. And as either of these notions of love is perverted or ignored, those who do so become less human.

These principles are clearly illustrated in the remaining days of this period (November 21-27). In his entry for November 21, Griffin reflects again on the inhumanity of day-to-day denials of basic conveniences to blacks — rest rooms, places to eat, water fountains. Here, as on many previous occasions, Griffin desperately cries that "it makes no sense." Why, he asks, does a whole society concentrate its efforts on denying black people the basic necessities of everyday living?

An answer of sorts comes from the foreman of a plant in Mobile where Griffin applies for a job. The answer is chilling, deadening in its sheer lack of reason, its sheer disregard for charity and humanitarian love. "We don't want you people," the foreman states flatly; in essence, he will do everything in his power to drive blacks out of the state. He will make life so difficult, so oppressive that blacks will have to leave — it's the only way to keep them out of white schools, restaurants, factories and businesses. The answer, then, is that an entire society has been brainwashed; it is completely and fundamentally racist, believing so firmly in the inferiority of Negroes that it has embarked on a well-organized campaign to stamp them out, as one would stamp out rats or malaria.

This racism is the result of a society's collective guilty conscience about slavery and various other forms of oppression. In its constant effort to repress this guilt, such a society has a vested interest in keeping black people in a status where it is impossible for them to exercise their full human rights and develop their full human abilities. The Southern white is trained by his society to play a role, the hypocrisy of which he cannot or does not acknowledge. He puts up to his fellow whites an image of graciousness, charm, and hospitality — a face Griffin remembers well from his visits to Mobile as a white man. The Southerner learns to make a great display of charitable love for his fellow man — with one glaring exception: he has been conditioned from birth simply to rule out Negroes as human beings and, therefore, as proper objects of love.

If the Mobile plant foreman is a parody and a perversion of humanitarian love, the driver Griffin meets on November 24 is a parallel case in his sexual attitudes. This man, a grandfather, a respected civic leader among whites, is a perfect example of the two different faces a Southerner has for blacks and for his own race. His sexual attitudes toward Negroes are the most blatant ones Griffin has so far encountered: black women are objects to satisfy the lust of white men; and if children result from such liaisons, it is doing them a favor to give them some white blood. This man, like so many Southerners Griffin has met, believes in "racial purity" only insofar as it means the preservation of the white race in an unadulterated state. (It is such a concept of "purity" which causes a white society to classify people who are one-quarter or one-eighth Negro as black rather than white, illogical though such reasoning may be.) However, probably the most shocking aspect of this man's character is the degree to which the hatred fostered by his racism can go. He warns Griffin that if he "stirs up trouble," he'll be "taken care of" — either by imprisonent or by murder.

As Griffin realizes that the desire to "teach a lesson" could become an unreasoning obsession with this man, he tries to visualize, by contrast, how the driver would appear among whites. There, he would be the "amiable, decent American" who would never let his family or friends see his desire for power over others, his need to cause pain. Such a man, such a paradox, preoccupies Griffin in some of his other writings. One of his best short stories, "The Cause," could have been about this particular Alabama grandfather — or the many others like him. Such men join the Ku Klux Klan, or gangs like the one which kidnapped Mack Parker, in order to convince themselves of their own importance and in order to stand as "heroes" among their fellow whites — guardians of the purity of their race and the purity of their women and children.

Griffin, in fact, had personal contact with one of the most tragic victims of men like this. In an interview in 1964 (see Daniel's article in the bibliography), Griffin described the shocking murder of a young man named Clyde Kennard. Kennard's only offense — besides being black — was trying to be admitted to a white university; he was arrested on trumped-up charges and sentenced to twenty-five years in prison for allegedly receiving twenty-five dollars worth of stolen chicken feed. He shortly developed intestinal cancer and was hospitalized. However, in 1962, when James Meredith entered the University of Mississippi, prison authorities decided to "make an example" of Kennard (who had no connection at all with Meredith) and took him from the hospital to serve on a sunup-to-sundown labor gang. As his illness grew worse, Kennard had to be carried out and back by his fellow prisoners. Finally, through the efforts of Martin Luther King, Jr., Dick Gregory, Griffin, and others, the dying man was released, the tragic victim of a society's compulsion to deny its own guilt. Yet, despite all that he had suffered, Kennard on his deathbed told Griffin that what had happened to him was not as bad as what had happened to the whites who had caused his death — and what would happen to their children; hatred had turned those whites, and would turn their children, into beasts.

Indeed, this Alabama grandfather and many like him were being encouraged by their racist society to see in their whole relationship to the Negro race a legitimate context for allowing themselves to drop all vestiges of their humanity and to allow their angry and sadistic and lustful urges full play. And the time would likely come in the lives of these men when they were no longer able to perceive which of their two faces was the "real" one. Was this grandfather *really* the good citizen and kindly family man with a blind spot about Negroes? Or was he *really* a sex fiend, a sadist, and a brute, who put up an acceptable front to white society? In other words, can a man's character be something apart from, and other than, the way in which he behaves toward certain other people?

Griffin does not actually pose such questions. Rather, with this grandfather, as many times before when confronting white racists, Griffin tries — as Kennard tried — not to lose the ability to see them as human beings, as victims of their society's distorted values, and ultimately as sick and warped personalities.

The day of November 24 closes, as did November 21, with an example of overwhelming love. But this example — a young

Alabama sawmill worker and his family — is deeply saddening because the situation seems so potentially hopeless. The young mill worker is constantly in debt despite his hard work: there is an organized effort by the white community to arrange that this man's bills will always slightly exceed his wages. He, his wife, and his six children are therefore forced to live in a two-room shack with no plumbing and only the most primitive furnishings. Yet in this abject poverty, the family has maintained bonds of love which alleviate their loneliness and need. Griffin thinks about the future of the children and sees only bleakness and disappointment. For the present, they and their parents can preserve a heroic optimism, but when the children are a little older, too many doors will be closed to them, and they will have to learn not to hope, not to trust.

Griffin tries to realize how he would feel if these were his own children, and he is immensely saddened. The loneliness and the despair that go along with being black in such a society, coupled with having to face prospects like these, overwhelm him. The remoteness of the house and the blackness of the night reinforce his sense of isolation. When he returns to the shack and is able to sleep, his fears and sense of hopelessness become nightmares of white men and women, their eyes burning with hatred, closing in on him so that there is no escape. In the morning, however, the kindness and the love of the black family reassure him, as did the views of the old black preacher a few days earlier. The wife's graciousness is in stark contrast both to her surroundings and to most of the whites Griffin has been encountering in the Deep South.

As he leaves the mill worker's shanty and heads for Montgomery, Griffin's feelings are reminiscent, in some ways, of his reactions and his sense of isolation just before he visited the Easts. Again, Griffin's escape lies in renewing his ties with familiar people and in planning a return to the white world. His feelings, as before, are complex and oppressive. He recalls after his nightmare that he had "begun this experiment in a spirit of scientific detachment," hoping to be objective, to keep his feelings out of it. As a matter of fact, Griffin had originally intended to write an analysis of life as a black man which would be of interest primarily to sociologists and psychologists, and which would involve little of a personal nature. But his feelings both conscious and unconscious, are now utterly engrossed by his experiences. He frequently feels guilt, anger, and sadness over the blindness of his fellow whites; simultaneously, he feels the isolation, frustration, anger, and hopelessness of being a black man in this racist society. It is fitting, therefore, that the whole section of his narrative from the visit with the Easts until now should center on the most basic human urges and emotions — sexual and humanitarian love.

Thus Griffin, oppressed by his emotions, goes into a phone booth and calls his wife. The conversation with her and his children momentarily takes him into a more comforting world — a world where a family's love is not tinged with despair, just as the booth itself shuts him off from what his surroundings mean to a black man. But he must return for a while to his blackness. As he first steps out into the lonely night, it seems to ally itself with him and comfort him. The lines of Langston Hughes' poem run through his mind. But the harsh realities of his second identity close in upon him as the light in the bus station reveals the hate stares of whites.

The last experience Griffin describes in any detail in this section is concerned with his impressions of the spirit of Martin Luther King, Jr. in Montgomery. King, of course, stood for all the principles Griffin was impressed by when he talked to the black leaders in New Orleans and to the old preacher in Mobile. King's philosophy was based on faith in the power of love, or charity, to prevail over hatred and racism through organized nonviolent action. As a result of the enactment of these policies in Montgomery, Griffin sees two somewhat conflicting tendencies. On the one hand, the Negroes' despair has yielded to determination; they have begun to hope that there really is a way to gain their rights and their dignity in white America, however slow the process. But on the other hand, the new stubbornness of blacks not only bewilders whites but also seems to make them afraid, defensive, more hostile — because for the first time it seems possible that they might have to back down, to abandon the fortress of their racism. As whites see it, the situation is, in essence, a battle to preserve the "Southern way of life"; their main fear is that the blacks may win.

On November 27, after three weeks as a black man, Griffin decides to pass back into white society. He will not totally abandon his black identity until December 14, but the effect of his medication is now sufficiently worn off to allow him again to pass as white. There seems to be two reasons for Griffin's decision to become a white man again. First, he finds the situation in Montgomery confusing and, as he noted in the entry for the previous day, he "could not make out the white viewpoint" in that city — a strange combination of apparent tolerance toward Negro advancement and an underlying sense of the "war" described above. Griffin implies that being a white man in Montgomery might allow him to understand this viewpoint better. Second, he is emotionally worn out by his experiences as a black man in the South, "sickened by the thought of any more hate." Therefore, he prepares once more to change his appearance and to retreat temporarily to his former identity.

PART V: PASSING BACK AND FORTH (MONTGOMERY, TUSKEGEE, CONYERS, AND ATLANTA; NOVEMBER 28-DECEMBER 14)

Griffin's disguise as a black man continues at times during these two and a half weeks, alternating with periods when he resumes his white identity. His journal entries during this period are somewhat disjointed, consisting of scattered impressions and reflections rather than a coherent narrative.

During this period of "zigzagging back and forth," Griffin's first experiences and thoughts center, appropriately enough, on the irrational difference in people's attitudes toward him simply because of a superficial change in skin color. When he appears to be white, he is smiled at by policemen, accepted without question in restaurants and public buildings, allowed to use any water fountain or rest room he wishes. White people on the streets turn friendly glances toward him and willingly engage in casual conversation.

The reactions of blacks to him as a white man are of two sorts. When he walks through a Negro section of town, the black teen-ager he meets is guarded and suspicious. On the other hand, the Negro bellhop in the Whitney Hotel puts on a false smile and the "eager to serve you, Massa" air which most whites demand. His servile manner is a barrier between him and Griffin; it presents to the journalist a stereotype which protects the black man from white hostility but, at the same time, effaces the bellhop's individuality and prevents personal communication between the two. Griffin observes these reactions and realizes that, despite the fact that he was taken to be black only one day earlier, the simple act of "passing over" into white society has cut him off from the confidence and trust of most blacks — not because he is a different person, and not because of any natural black hostility to whites, but because Southern racism has made Negroes fearful, suspicious, and aware of the wisdom — in fact, the necessity — of keeping their individual personalities invisible to white society.

Griffin's past experiences, however, have shown him that the need for playing such a role, while humiliating to the black man, has not made all Negroes into abject Uncle Toms. One of the next incidents in this section reveals Griffin's increased understanding of the black man's perspective. The episode with the bellhop is followed fairly closely in the narrative by the journalist's account of the incident in the Montgomery bus station where he appears as a Negro. When the overbearing woman sees Griffin, she reacts in a thoroughly racist way: Griffin is a "nigger" and, therefore, a servant, an underling, who must obey her commands. But Griffin's actions — at first apparently demeaning to him — have a double effect. On the one hand, we see Griffin being referred to as a "boy." We immediately see a parallel in the bellhop in the Whitney Hotel. He too is a man deserving of much more dignified treatment and employment, but America's racism prevents whites from knowing him for the man that he is. On the other hand, however, we see that Griffin has a moral victory. The woman's racism makes her into a caricature, and Griffin takes full advantage of her narrowmindedness to emphasize her dehumanizing bigotry. She expects Griffin to fawn upon her, to fall at her feet in his eagerness to serve her — and so Griffin does just that, a little *too* enthusiastically. His grinning servility mocks her haughtiness. The woman senses the mockery but cannot really do much about it; her society does not allow her to behave as a person, a human being dealing with another human being, but demands that she act in the role of a Southern white dealing with a "nigger" — and a Southern white cannot imagine having to tell a black man that he is behaving *too* humbly, *too* abjectly. Thus Griffin, without once failing to "keep in his place" allows the woman's racism to frustrate and embarrass her.

The journalist's next meeting with a white person involves more complex issues and is more saddening to the writer. The white man who identifies himself as a Ph.D. from New York represents some unfortunate, misguided aspects of "white liberalism" in America. In contrast to Griffin's own motives for learning about the plight of blacks in the South and his way of approaching the project, the Ph.D. has chosen the role of an "observer," and he obviously wishes not so much to learn about the specific problems of Negroes or the actual facts of their oppression as to be accepted and praised for his generous concern in "coming all the way from New York" to show his "brotherhood."

The man is not malicious; he is simply misguided and unconsciously, cloddishly, condescending. He does not realize that he is treating the Negroes whom he meets not as brothers — that is, as human beings just like himself — but as members of a group which depends like children on his aid, his concern. He has the kind of "missionary" attitude which so often produces tension between well-intentioned, but imperceptive, white teachers or social workers and the ghetto residents they become involved with in their work. The basic assumption of such a pose is that blacks are unfortunate, uninformed people with certain natural limitations, who could not — even if given the freedom rightly theirs—really manage without the paternal guidance of whites.

The Ph.D. implies such an evaluation of Negroes in his patronizing efforts to buy all the turkeys an elderly vendor is trying to sell. Outright philanthropy like this usually implies some kind of condescension. Moreover, apart from his condescension, a second mistake in the New Yorker's action is that it ignores the main issues involved in what he sees. The circumstances which force this elderly man to ride about selling his turkeys in order to scrape together enough to live cannot be changed by a gift which temporarily relieves his poverty. Buying up the turkeys is no solution to the problem; its main benefit is to the giver rather than to the receiver; he feels himself to be generous and kind.

If the New Yorker were perceptive enough, he would realize what the old vendor is trying to say to him when he rejects his offer. The old man, first of all, refuses to accept the Ph.D. as a generous benefactor, someone above him. Instead he treats him as an equal — and tries to point out that accepting the money would, in a sense, be taking unfair advantage of a fellow human being. Furthermore, the vendor emphasizes the fact that the Northerner does not need and cannot use the turkeys. This clearly suggests that the problem is not that individual white men are not generous enough, but that white society as a whole has structured its economy so as to keep Negroes from being necessary in any but a few selected menial tasks. Such is the "system": the white Ph.D. does not need the old black man's turkeys, but many poor Negroes do need the food. The Ph.D., however, is not really interested enough or farsighted enough to discover what he might constructively do about discrimination and poverty. He would probably find burdensome any long-term commitment to changing fundamentally his own attitudes and those of his friends, to reforming political and economic structures so as to make black people essential parts of the society, and fighting against the underlying causes of specific racial injustices. Instead, when the vendor refuses his money, the New Yorker takes this as a rejection of white efforts toward "understanding," rather than seeing the situation as it really is. He thinks there is "something funny" about Negroes because they aren't overwhelmed with gratitude toward him and other white "liberals." It is impossible for him to conceive that the turkey vendor is a man whose intelligence, pride, and dignity are offended by the implications of his offer, but who nevertheless conceals his hurt and indignation in order to treat the white man courteously.

This incident is especially discouraging to Griffin because it shows all too clearly how wide the gap is between the attitudes of Northern liberals – the strongest supporters of legislative reform – and a true sense of equality and brotherhood, free of condescension and awkwardness. If this is, except for isolated individuals, the "better side" of white men; if, as the Ph.D. asserts, ". . . people like me . . . are your only hope," how far whites still have to go. And how little hope there seems to be that true communication and understanding between the races will be achieved soon enough to prevent further bloody repression of blacks or militant uprisings by a people too long oppressed.

On the bus to Atlanta, Griffin meets another white who obviously considers himself "enlightened," but whose hypocrisy speaks considerably more clearly than his words. The incident which introduces him to Griffin occurs when two Negroes are asked to share a seat so that two white women can sit down without having to be next to a black. The Negroes' refusal to do so almost causes a white bully to start a fight with them. The "white liberal" in question asserts – after the incident is over – that he would have taken the blacks' side if the bully had struck them. But Griffin is wise to the ways of the self-styled liberal by now. Why, he asks us, didn't the man make his views known when the danger was greatest? Isn't he simply seeking the same approval of his "enlightened outlook" which the Ph.D. so desired?

Proof of the shallowness of the man's convictions comes when he calls the threatened black man "boy." Like the Ph.D., he does not realize that true brotherhood cannot be achieved by paternalism. A man who says he is your brother but who obviously regards you as inferior is lying either to you or to himself. The latter type, the kind of self-deceiving racist who asserts (as both the Ph.D. and the man on the bus might) that "some of my best friends are Negroes" is in many senses the most frustrating white for blacks to encounter. This is true because this white man is better intentioned than the overt bigot and cannot as easily be hated or written off as incapable of change; in addition, this white man seems at times to offer hope to black people, yet ends up, in effect, leaving only slightly ajar doors which had in the past been shut. He may, for example, offer Negroes integrated high schools, but, unable to overcome his stereotype of them as intellectually inferior, he will channel all but a token few black students into non-academic programs which will not qualify them for college. He may even invite a well-spoken black lawyer or physician into his home, but he will unthinkingly make his guest acutely uncomfortable by showing him off to his white friends as proof of his liberal views. In short, he still regards it as the exception, rather than the rule, that a black man could be as intelligent as he, hold a comparable job, or be "acceptable" in the social circles in which he travels.

His contact with so-called white liberals, who are supposedly the only hope of Negroes, is so disheartening to Griffin that he seeks a kind of refuge in a colored rest room. With deliberate irony, Griffin draws a comparison between the rest room and a medieval church. In the Middle Ages, churches were regarded as sacred, safe from attack or siege, even in wartime. A wanderer or wounded man could seek sanctuary in a church and be safe from his enemies as long as he remained there. Now, on the battleground of racial conflict, a Negro toilet cubicle becomes a precious sanctuary — one of the few places a black can be sheltered from white hatred.

Griffin's feelings of being protected in a small enclosed space are similar to those late on November 24 when he shut himself in a phone booth to call his wife and children. At that time, the booth had been an escape and a consolation; when he stepped out, the beauty of the night also sheltered and reassured him for a short time. Here, the rest room is sheltering in a more sinister way. Griffin is reminded not only of a medieval church (which suggests the bloody battles waged around the church as well as the sanctuary the building provided) but also of a coffin. The implication seems to be that there are times when the only true sanctuary, the only true escape, for the black man in a racist society is death. Perhaps here, for the first time, Griffin fully understands the feelings behind the cold statistics which he had studied as his book began — the increase in the number of Negroes who did not care whether they lived or died.

Yet Griffin's view of what it means to be black has changed in other ways during his weeks as a Negro. We recall that his first impressions of himself as a black man were almost entirely negative — he saw blackness only in terms of a joyless, oppressive existence, victimized by white racism. His moments in the rest room briefly recall this point of view — but only briefly. Griffin has seen many other aspects of blackness: the sense of brotherhood and kindness toward one another, the dedication to decency and lovingness despite the obstacles, the dignified and patient persistence to obtain basic rights in the face of irrational opposition. He has also learned some of the ways in which a black can get the last laugh on whites by utilizing the very grotesqueness of their bigotry — as in the incident when his servile gratitude mocked the haughtiness of the woman who ordered him to carry her bags in the bus station.

Thus, when Griffin steps forth from the rest room a white man once again, his relief at dropping his disguise and the tensions that go with it is mingled with regret. One specific limitation of his resumed identity immediately comes to him: his speech as a white man must now be guarded and restrained; he cannot lapse into the relaxed and friendly "semiobscene" language he has become accustomed to as a Negro.

This specific, and seemingly insignificant, limitation is undoubtedly mentioned by Griffin here not because it is his only regret but because it stands for a whole pattern of white thinking and behavior to which he is not eager to return. Southern white society so thoroughly rejects all other races and cultures that they have become strained, uneasy, "uptight" and inhibited in their behavior to all whom they perceive to be "different" from themselves. The barriers which whites set up produce corresponding defenses on the part of blacks. So Griffin, as a returning member of white society, will no longer be let in on the humor and friendliness he found so appealing as a black man among blacks. Moreover, if he does happen to overhear Negroes joking among themselves, his role as a white man in the eyes of other whites demands that he repress any natural inclination he may have to grin or laugh at their pleasantries.

There is an underlying principle here which has been involved in several of Griffin's experiences and reflections elsewhere in the book; namely, that prejudice and discrimination harm not only those who are their objects but also their practitioners. We have seen how a "hate stare" brutalizes the one who gives it at least as much as it insults the person at whom it is directed. We have also seen how the sexual attitudes of some racist whites distort their own values as much as they debase and stereotype blacks. Griffin's thoughts here emphasize how many of the white man's day-to-day reactions must be limited, inhibited, or dehumanized in order to conform to the "rules" of the cruel game of racism—cruel because ultimately there are no winners, only losers on both sides. But the white man is still far from perceiving this fact.

Indeed, nothing more clearly illustrates the amount of energy and concentration demanded of the white man's "role" than the behavior of the bus driver described in Griffin's entry for December 2. He must keep careful watch on his speech so that each white leaving the bus is told to watch his step and each Negro is denied this courtesy. A simple occurrence like the bunching together of whites and blacks causes him a good amount of anxiety: how can he manage both to be polite to all the whites and yet avoid acting like a "nigger lover" in their eyes by extending his politeness to the black woman getting off at the same stop? How much simpler, freer, less "uptight" his life would be if he did not have to concern himself with such things.

The events of December 2 through December 14 involve three distinct areas of concentration: first, a resumption of

Griffin's reflections on religion and racism; second, his impressions of progress in Atlanta; and third, a final incident emphasizing the barriers to simple interaction between individual blacks and whites.

Griffin's visit to the Trappist monastery in Conyers, Georgia, is a kind of retreat — a time of meditation and contemplation on the role of religion in overcoming racism. Like all retreats, it is a departure from the everyday routine in an attempt to achieve a better and deeper perspective. Griffin finds in the Trappist guestmaster a spokesman for an ideal of Christianity, a man who insists on a scholarly and careful interpretation of religious dogmas and who denies the right of men to bend these dogmas or distort the Scriptures in order to find support for their own bigotry or hatred.

Griffin's questions to the monk emphasize the fact that a majority of the Southern churches he has observed consistently violate or ignore this ideal. Racism has penetrated not only politics and economics but also religion. Thus, a person like the young college English teacher, whom Griffin meets here, finds that sharing the convictions of people like the Trappist guestmaster means being cut off from home and family — presumably, under the circumstances of the young man's being at the monastery, a Christian family who sees no inconsistencies between their religious beliefs and their society's racism.

But, as the contemporary French philosopher Jacques Maritain points out, the God whom racists invoke is a total perversion of the God of the true Christian faith. Griffin obviously agrees with the French thinker that a racist God, a God who doubles as the supreme Ku Klux Klansman or white supremacist is not a God but a projection of men's need to be reinforced in their own distorted values. Such a God, Griffin's reflections imply, is as much a false object of devotion as the golden idols condemned in the Old Testament. And just as human beings were slaughtered on the altars of the biblical idols, so whole races and cultures are still being victimized in the name of the Southern racists' God.

Griffin leaves the Trappist monastery to fulfill an assignment for *Sepia* – a report on Negro leaders in Atlanta. The journalist firmly states that the situation in Atlanta has shown him that the outlook for change is not utterly hopeless. In contrast to the situation in Montgomery, Griffin finds not only optimism and persistence among Negroes but also real evidence of political and economic progress achieved by the unified efforts of black people.

For Griffin as a journalist, the importance of the press in such a process of change cannot be overlooked. Thus one of the first hopeful signs he notes in Atlanta is the presence of a newspaper which is not afraid to speak out for racial justice and equality. Griffin digresses somewhat to praise certain outstanding Southern journalists and to condemn newspapers which are intimidated by threats of advertisers and by the Ku Klux Klan and Citizens Councils into suppressing everything favorable to blacks and playing on the racist sympathies of their subscribers. Griffin obviously views the role of the press as one not of conforming to public opinion but of helping to influence it in a responsible way through fair editorial policies and conscientious reporting of facts. Such a belief, in fact, must have been a major reason for Griffin's publication of this book.

The most important signs of Atlanta's progress, however, are found in the actual achievements of its Negroes. First of all, blacks are beginning to exert some economic control over business, industry, and banking. This control originated, Griffin tells us, with the efforts of two black economists, Milton and Blayton, to pool the resources of the black community in order to establish banks and lending agencies. (Similar cooperative efforts are occurring at the present time in a number of areas of the country.)

The importance of the economic influence gained through such cooperatives is well illustrated by Griffin's account of an incident involving the buying of homes by Negroes. In the typical Southern city or town, blacks who wish to purchase houses in white sections, even in the unusual case when they might have the consent of most white residents in the area, can be prevented from doing so by the refusal of white-controlled banks and agencies to grant loans. In the case described, however, the establishment of black lending agencies not only allowed a few Negroes to procure the necessary loans but also created a competitive economic situation which caused white agencies, afraid of losing out on profits, to make additional loans available. Without the actual competition from black agencies, though, white cooperation would not have been forthcoming.

A second area of significant black progress in Atlanta is education. The leadership and intellectual achievement of the administrators and scholars whom Griffin names give dramatic evidence that the theories of Negro intellectual inferiority are totally false. Nevertheless, Griffin must realize that black scholars and scientists are too often entirely unknown to the very whites for whom such myths need to be disproved. In fact, most well-educated whites reading this list today must feel embarrassment at how few of the names are familiar to them; so-called world history texts still devote little space to countries dominated by non-white cultures, and American history books generally omit the achievements of all but a very few of the country's black citizens.

Yet another myth is disproven by the achievements of Atlanta's Negroes: the well-established misconception that any movement of blacks into a residential area automatically causes the neighborhood to deteriorate. The precise reasons why such a pattern has often appeared to hold true are complex and disputed even by experts. However some of the causes are surely related to whites' economic exploitation of blacks. In one typical pattern, a white homeowner might be convinced by realtors or speculators that the value of his property would soon depreciate because blacks were planning to move into his neighborhood. This man might sell out quickly and cheaply to the realtor or speculator. The new landlord would then divide the house into as many apartments as possible for rental to Negroes. The chronic lack of inexpensive apartments in most cities would allow this landlord to be assured of renting his units without properly maintaining them. Thus the property, though profitable to its owner, would deteriorate—not primarily because of the habits of its tenants, but because of the failure of the landlord to comply with even the most basic health and building standards. In many cases, a landlord, by buying property cheaply and dividing it into many units, can make a considerable profit even while paying fines for building code violations.

The situation in Atlanta stands in complete contrast to this kind of pattern. Because successful blacks themselves have gained control over significant amounts of real estate, they have been able to sell properties at fair prices to other blacks, supplying loans at reasonable interest rates. Thus both the exploitation involved in renting from white landlords and the financial disadvantages of renting, as opposed to owning property, has been somewhat eliminated.

Finally, Griffin discusses black political influence in Atlanta. As opposed to many areas of the South he has described in earlier parts of this book—for example, Poplarville, Mississippi, site of the Mack Parker murder—this Georgia city is not a place where most Negroes have to live in fear of physical harm or loss of jobs for registering to vote. Moreover, black voting strength has been consolidated enough to elect the first Negro public official in the state since the era of reconstruction after the Civil War. The influence of black voters is obviously seen in the fair policies of Mayor Hartsfield. In a very rare situation in Southern politics, the mayor discovered that his winning of the black vote was sufficient to balance out his loss of the white racist vote. Thus he could pursue his ideals of fairness and still receive sufficient public support.

The last few days when Griffin passes as a black involve the white photographer Don Rutledge, first in Atlanta, then in New Orleans. Griffin introduces us to Rutledge's reactions at the end of the December 7 entry; the photographer's general impressions seem to sum up Griffin's own total response to the Southern black experience: concern for the incredible oppression of many Negroes' lives, humiliation at the extent to which white society is racist; and finally a sense of delight in the brotherliness, the humor and patience and tenderness of black life which outweighs the other negative reactions. Rutledge does, however, find that the long-standing barriers between the races originally erected by whites are not easily crossed by either white or black. His attempts to photograph Negroes arouse suspicion and fear. And he. begins to realize how his companionship with Griffin, now disguised as a black man, places limitations on his use of rest rooms and eating places.

In the last entry of this section, December 14, Griffin reiterates the feelings he had when he temporarily returned to his white identity. He ends, as Rutledge does, with a positive as well as a negative idea of what it is like to be black in a society hostile to one's color. He feels a strange sadness in leaving the Negro world, which he describes as ceasing to share blacks' "pain and heartache." But he also has previously expressed sadness at no longer sharing the humor and ease of blacks' relationships with one another. Perhaps Griffin senses that, in a society dominated by whites whose prejudice has had a progressively dehumanizing influence, being black is more painful but it is also more human, in the fullest sense, than being a racist white.

EPILOGUE: THE FATE OF A "NIGGER LOVER" (MANSFIELD, TEXAS, AND ELSEWHERE; DECEMBER 15-AUGUST 17)

This "epilogue of sorts" is intended to show the varieties of white reactions to Griffin's project. The section is very loosely organized into three divisions: Griffin's initial reactions to his return home and his preparations for publication; the favorable national and international reactions to the news of his project; and the local, adverse response and threats of violence, which eventually force the Griffin family to leave Texas.

The journalist's initial sensations upon his return home highlight once more the theme of love. The warmth of his wife and children, and of his parents, reassure him that they are on his side; their love contrasts strongly with the bigotry Griffin has so frequently encountered in the past weeks and with the adverse reactions he expects to encounter. To Griffin it seems that such loving kindness should be the antidote to racism; how can men oppress other men if they truly know how to love, how to give to others, he asks. The question evokes the young white construction worker whose love for his family flowed outward into tolerance for all men (November 19); at the opposite extreme, the question recalls the Alabama grandfather who was a so-called model citizen and devoted family man among whites, but whose racism was so acute that it threatened to erupt in violence (November 24). Griffin, recalling both, asks why there is no correlation between love for individuals and love for all men. But he is unable to supply any answer because of his recent experiences.

The meeting with George Levitan and Mrs. Jackson of *Sepia* reiterates the fears for his family's safety which are already in Griffin's mind, but reaffirms his commitment to make his experiences known. Griffin tells us of his reasons for publishing parts of his journal (later incorporated into *Black Like Me*) in this magazine. Basically, he wished to let its readers, almost all of whom would be Negroes, know that someone cared and was trying to understand. We may assume, however, from the emphasis of *Black Like Me* in its present form, that this longer account would be more important as a means of changing white opinions.

The fact that Griffin had lived briefly as a black man first becomes widely known on March 14. For the rest of that month, Griffin's descriptions of public reactions center on the sympathetic response of news media and prominent television figures to his experiences. In the early 1960s, television interview programs were gaining great popularity. The three interviewers on whose shows Griffin appears were among the most prominent in the country: Dave Garroway, Mike Wallace, and Paul Coates. And all three prove to be immensely sympathetic. Griffin's apprehensions about the two New York shows vary according to the public images of the interviewers. With Garroway, Griffin fears he will be asked to play down any unpleasant aspects of his experiences. On the other hand, in meeting Wallace, a man noted for his sharp tongue and relentlessness in backing prominent figures into corners, the Texan is afraid that too much will be probed at and revealed, that the identities of people who could be victimized may be disclosed. In each case his fears prove to be groundless. The same favorable response occurs on an international level when a French television show features Griffin's experiences.

But local reactions are of a very different sort. On March 17, only three days after the Coates interview is broadcast, Griffin's mother receives a hate call and threats against her son. Thus there begins for Griffin and his family a period of isolation from most of their neighbors, of living under police protection, a time when the few real friends like the Joneses and the Turners repeatedly show their courage and loyalty.

Griffin's journalistic eye focuses on a series of briefly described episodes which capture perfectly the uncertainties and fears, the confused emotions he feels during this period. The hostility of his fellow townsmen in Mansfield is alternately a source of grim humor and of fear for the journalist. A sign on a local cafe — "No Albinos Allowed" — implies, not without crude wit, that all these years Griffin had really been a Negro with a deficiency in pigmentation which enabled him to pass for white. Griffin's amusement at the cafe owner's racist wit recalls the humor with which P. D. East confronted the insanities of hatred and prejudice. On the other hand, the episode of hanging Griffin in effigy on Main Street points up dramatically just how little support was given him by local authorities and by the majority of townspeople. The police obviously chose to look the other way when the "hanging" occurred. And the failure of the townspeople to condemn the outrage speaks eloquently of the combined fear and racism which inhibit their human sympathies and cut off their friendliness. In the context of such an abnormal situation, the grocer's decision to act just as he always had toward Griffin's father becomes an act of heroism.

The thoughts Griffin records in his journal during these tense and apprehensive days strongly reinforce his conviction that what he has done is a thoroughly reasonable action and that the society which condemns it and rejects him is unsound and irrational in its values. He notes, for example, that the women of the town are debating whether or not his masquerade was a "Christian" thing (April 1), and that most townspeople wanted to "keep things peaceful" at all costs (April 11). Griffin's own convictions are clear: we know that he believes that silence in the face of injustice is deeply and fundamentally un-Christian; he states explicitly that being "peaceful" in the sense the people of Mansfield mean is destroying the only real peace—that based on a society in which all men can rely on the goodwill of their fellow men.

Griffin's situation at this point is almost a classic one—that of a man whose decision to follow the course of action his conscience has designated as morally right has caused total rejection by his fellow men. The concept that a man's most profound decisions must be based on inner convictions rather than on popular values and the corresponding notion that every person is, in this sense, a "loner" are basic to Griffin's values. His novel *Nuni*, for example, deals with the process by which a "civilized" man, alone in an isolated and supposedly much more primitive society, gradually strips away the superficialities of his own background to come to grips with his most basic values. Griffin's own experiences, like those of the hero of his novel, seem to tell us that even presumably civilized societies are in many senses primitive, hostile, full of taboos and suspicions, and that a moral man, in order to find his own peace, must inevitably reject many of his society's values and must be rejected by its members.

But few men have the courage to take a public stance and to face its consequences. The overwhelmingly favorable mail Griffin receives convinces him, as he says (June 19), that the "average Southern white" is much less bigoted than the overall voice of his society, but does not make his views known for fear of reprisals or rejection by his racist neighbors. Griffin, having taken such a stand overtly, is eventually unable to remain geographically within this society which threatens his life. The dangers to his family are too great.

As he leaves to join his wife, parents, and children in Mexico, Griffin is not defeated by his society's racism—but neither has he won any tangible victories over it. His experiences have undoubtedly deepened his own perception and solidified his convictions. Accordingly, any victories over prejudice which may result from the publication of his account will be personal, private ones on the part of his readers, inner moral modifications rather than rapid and sweeping changes in public opinion or practice. All that he can hope is that if enough people individually grow and change, sooner or later the loud voices of the fanatical racists will fall upon deaf ears and their influence will eventually be nullified by the force of the popular vote. Such a patient, long-term plan, as we shall see below, is consistent with Griffin's overall outlook at the time when he was writing *Black Like Me.*

GRIFFIN'S PHILOSOPHY: 1960 AND AFTER

Throughout *Black Like Me,* one thing is quite clear about John Howard Griffin's values and philosophy: he, as a committed Roman Catholic, firmly believes that the ideal of Christian love *(caritas)*, if truly put into practice by churches and by individuals, would eliminate bigotry, prejudice, and racism. In this book, such a belief is reflected in the philosophies of those whom Griffin most admires, from the French philosopher Jacques Maritain, to the elderly black preacher who claims that the only way in which the white man can destroy Negroes is to make them lose their ability to love and forgive their oppressors. "If we hated them," he declares, "we'd be sunk down to their level."

Such a concept of the power of love is behind the New Orleans Ministerial Alliance to desegregate buses (November 8); and it was the basis of Martin Luther King, Jr.'s nonviolent resistance against discrimination in Montgomery (November 25) and elsewhere. Moreover, this ideal of love is by no means limited to clergymen, philosophers, or even to Christians. Both the white construction worker, who gives Griffin a ride in Alabama (November 19), and the young black sawmill worker and his family (November 24) exemplify a kind of love which extends to all their relationships with people, regardless of race. In neither case does Griffin allude to their religion.

Griffin's basic values, then, center on humanitarian love, peace, and nonviolence. At the time of this book, he believed that persistent, dignified resistance and the education of the public through the news media and other means could ultimately put an end to racism and achieve equality for all people. He emphatically rejected Negro movements toward militancy or separatism: in the last entry (August 17), Griffin speaks with dismay of a "rise in racism among Negroes"; he believed that some blacks' drives for vengeance or their rejection of all white men would only lead them into "the same tragic error the white racist has made."

If Griffin were writing *Black Like Me* today, would he condemn the general trend toward militancy which has developed among some blacks in the last ten years? Would he deplore as senseless violence or as the work of black racists the riots of Newark or Watts?

Although Griffin has published very little since 1960, certain clear modifications in his attitude have shown themselves in a number of magazine interviews. In 1964, for example, Griffin, talking to Bradford Daniel (see bibliography), called the Black Muslims a racist organization, but placed the blame for their growth on whites. Negroes, he stated, could no longer trust whites to act in good conscience: ". . . if this country lived up to its principles, we wouldn't have any Black Muslims." Griffin added that as long as even the more liberal whites continue to be appallingly unaware and to think in terms of "giving" Negroes rights—as though rights were the white man's to confer—and as long as whites fail to live up to their ideals in specific cases, black resentment and frustration will continue to grow.

On the subject of ghetto riots and race riots, Griffin testifies from a certain amount of personal experience since his assignments as a reporter several times have led him to thorough investigations of areas where such confrontations have taken place. In an exchange of letters with Sarah Patton Boyle, a longtime friend (see bibliography), he states that in each case with which he is familiar, he has discovered that there has been deliberate provocation of riots by white racist groups. Furthermore, Griffin has testified to the fact that blacks are overwhelmingly more often the victims of violence than its initiators. Policemen, Griffin believes, often act brutally toward Negroes, not so much out of conscious malice as out of the unconscious acceptance of white racist values (see Krebs' article in the bibliography). Nor is such repression limited to the South, according to Griffin: "I have seen the same brutality in New York City that I have seen in Mississippi. . . . the same lack of communication between Negro and white citizens in Cleveland, Detroit, Los.Angeles, Rochester, and Buffalo that I have seen in Alabama" (see Griffin's "Racist Sins of Christians" in the bibliography).

All in all, Griffin's perspective has changed considerably since 1960. He has witnessed the failure of most of the tactics he then espoused: education of the public, dissemination of facts about racist practices, and efforts of churches to put into practice the ideal of love for one's fellow man. In his interview with Krebs, in fact, Griffin explicitly admitted that if he had written *Black Like Me* in 1968 instead of 1960, it would have been very different.

Moreover, although Griffin has never espoused the initiation of violent action as a tactic for achieving change, he has spoken out quite strongly in some recent interviews. Basically, his view seems to be that while he deplores all violence, white America, by failing to respond to nonviolent tactics — except in the most temporary and limited ways — has left Negroes no alternative. Griffin believes that most blacks share his own regret that they have been driven to militancy; he tells Krebs: "The conclusions drawn, and often very reluctantly, by great numbers of Negro citizens are simply that nothing works. We are at a stalemate, children are growing up damaged, and it is better to destroy the whole structure."

When Griffin wrote the last sentences of *Black Like Me*, he foresaw the possibilities of violent racial confrontations and warned that they would result only in "a senseless tragedy of ignorant against ignorant, injustice answering injustice — a holocaust that will drag down the innocent and right-thinking masses of human beings." By 1968, when he was interviewed by Krebs, Griffin had evidently lost his faith that the masses were "right-thinking"; he had ceased to believe that those who urged militant action against injustice were themselves unjust or ignorant; he had concluded that the tragedies which would almost surely result from open rebellion could no longer be perceived as more senseless than those already involved in the day-to-day experiences of the oppressed.

REVIEW QUESTIONS

1. What are Griffin's reactions to his first view of himself as a black man? Why does he feel so lonely, so alienated from his new identity? How may his feelings have been affected by the values of Southern white society?

2. What does Griffin learn about the blacks' ideas of brotherhood from his experiences and conversations with the man in the shower (November 7)? with the men in the Y Cafe? with Sterling, Joe, and the wino? with the sawmill worker's family?

3. How do Griffin's own experiences as a black man prepare him to understand Christophe's rage and frustration? Explain the forces which are probably responsible for the formation of Christophe's character.

4. What is meant by racism? What are some of the historical forces and events which have encouraged the growth and continuation of racism in the South?

5. Distinguish some of the varieties of white racism which Griffin encounters. Which whites are the most vicious? the most saddening and frustrating?

6. Explain Griffin's reactions to the white racists he meets. Why does he feel pity rather than hatred toward them?

7. What is Griffin's idea of *caritas* or humanitarian love? Who are some of the people he meets who best exemplify this kind of love?

8. What does Griffin see as the role of the Christian religion — or any religion — in dealing with racial injustice? How well have the churches and individual Christians Griffin encountered lived up to this ideal?

9. What is the importance of P. D. East to the narrative? What are his outstanding character traits?

10. Explain the importance and significance of certain objects which Griffin makes into symbols of his attitudes at various times: darkness and nighttime; small enclosed spaces, such as phone booths and toilet cubicles; blank film negatives and burned-out light bulbs. Select scenes in which Griffin focuses attention on certain objects in order to help us visualize or experience his feelings vividly.

11. Describe the Southern racist view of Negroes' sexual drives and general level of morality. Among the whites and Negroes whom Griffin meets, who seems to have the more distorted sexual values?

12. In view of Griffin's experiences, how valid is the Southern white's idea that Negroes like things as they are or that Negroes lack the finer sensibilities, tastes, and emotions of white men?

13. Explain the nature of the progress which Griffin found in Atlanta. Why was economic growth and independence so important in achieving some of these improvements?

14. Explain the philosophy of Martin Luther King, Jr. and describe the spirit of Negro civil rights protest in the 1950s and at the time when Griffin was writing this book. How has the emphasis of black protest changed in the last ten years?

15. How did Griffin feel about growing black militancy at the time when he wrote *Black Like Me?* What did he most fear? How have his views changed since then?

SELECTED BIBLIOGRAPHY

Other Major Works by Griffin

GRIFFIN, JOHN HOWARD. *The Devil Rides Outside.* Fort Worth: Smits, Inc., 1952.

———. *Land of the High Sky.* Midland, Texas: First National Bank of Midland, 1959.

———. *Nuni.* Boston: Houghton Mifflin Co., 1956.

———. "Scattered Shadows," *Ramparts,* I, No. 4 (January, 1963), 18-35. A selection from his forthcoming autobiography.

———. *The John Howard Griffin Reader.* With photographs by the author. Selected and edited by Bradford Daniel. Boston: Houghton Mifflin Co., 1968. Includes in whole, or in part, all of Griffin's major works, a number of his articles and short stories, plus valuable background material and criticism.

Recent Articles and Interviews

DANIEL, BRADFORD, and JOHN HOWARD GRIFFIN. "Why They Can't Wait: An Interview with a White Negro," *The Progressive,* XXVIII, No. 7 (July, 1964), 15-19. Griffin's comments on the immorality of whites' "gradualism" in acknowledging Negroes' rights, on growing black disillusionment and militancy, and on the tragic death of Clyde Kennard.

GRIFFIN, JOHN HOWARD. "Racist Sins of Christians," *Sign,* XLIII, No. 1 (August, 1963), 7-10. Reprinted in *The John Howard Griffin Reader.* The failure of churches to work effectively against racism.

————, and SARAH PATTON BOYLE. "The Racial Crisis: An Exchange of Letters," *Christian Century*, LXXXV (May 22, 1968), 679-83. Griffin's response to the fears of black militancy voiced by Miss Boyle, a white participant in the early civil rights movement.

KREBS, A. V., JR. "A Visit with John Howard Griffin," *U.S. Catholic*, XXXIV (October, 1968), 28-32. Griffin's speculations about how he would have written *Black Like Me* in 1968, his comments on the failure of churches to take the lead in achieving racial justice, and his evaluation of the circumstances behind race riots.

MCDONNELL, THOMAS P. "John Howard Griffin: An Interview," *Ramparts*, I, No. 4 (January, 1963), 7-17. Griffin's discussion of some of the motives behind his disguise as a black man.

Criticism of Griffin's Works

GEISMAR, MAXWELL. "John Howard Griffin: The Devil in Texas," in *American Moderns*. New York: Hill and Wang, 1958. Reprinted in *The John Howard Griffin Reader*. A good introduction to the range of Griffin's writing and an assessment of his importance as a writer of fiction.

RANK, HUGH. "The Rhetorical Effectiveness of *Black Like Me*," *English Journal*, LVII (September, 1968), 813-17. An analysis of the literary devices and general structure of the book.

NOTES